SERVICE UNUSUAL

How Service Leaders Look Beyond the Obvious to Find Success

George T.K. Quek

First Published 2005

Published and distributed by:
Rank Books
Blk 1002, Toa Payoh Ind Pk #07-1423 Singapore 319074

Tel: (65) 6250 8180   Fax: (65) 6250 6191
Website: www.rankbooks.com   Email: admin@rankbooks.com

ISBN 981-05-3731-X

Printed In Singapore

What Others Say

"Not everyone would be as humble as the author to share about his [negative] spirit of pride and how he has learnt from that experience as part of the introduction to the book. More than providing some practical service unusual practices, this book talks about the heart of service - the service provider's heart. Though the author talks about the need to provide unusual service, what's really unusual is the need to connect the service that he/she provides to Servant Leadership. Not many people like this term because it demands that the reader reflect on the deeper intentions of his/her own heart. It might take an unusual reader to pick up this book. Put the author's tips into practice and your customers will walk away delighted and start thinking about how he/she could also provide an unusual experience to others."

Ernest Lee, Deputy Director (Training & Knowledge Management), Inland Revenue of Singapore

"George Quek has provided the most insightful treatise yet on customer service quality. *Service Unusual* is a masterpiece that goes beyond popular beliefs about customer service. The central message of this book is simple yet compelling: if we are always doing what others are doing, then we will never become superior performers. With an impressive background that bridges the East and the West, the author provides us with rich examples of unusual service practices from both sides of the globe. Unequivocally, this book is a must read for all leaders, managers and executives seeking to bring their organizations to the highest levels of success in today's competitive world. Even scholars and academics will benefit tremendously from the lessons in this book."

Dr. Peng Chan, Professor of Management, California State University-Fullerton, and President, Global Management Group

"Two out of three people in Hong Kong today are employed in service-related industries, and yet most people rarely learn what true service is. *Service Unusual* highlights the growing importance of service companies in today's economy and touches all the bases needed to develop quality and customer satisfaction in a service business. This book shows clearly the critical distinction between copycat service and services that really stand out in today's economy.

Written in 9 accessible chapters from the 'grounds up' and by skilfully blending theory, experience and examples throughout, the author offers a clear picture of each of the unconventional service practices required to develop quality service successfully. The concepts and tools which the author puts forth in this book are not just theoretical, ivory tower ideas, but actually work in practice.

Service Unusual is a required read for any executive in the service-related industry, regardless of how well they think their company might be doing. This is a dynamic, highly competitive world without national borders. This book is especially helpful for executives who are formulating a service strategy to compete in today's changing world economy."

David Ng, Human Resource Manager, Hong Kong Convention & Exhibition Centre

"In line with the service unusual principles of George's book, Nok Air has established ourselves very clearly as an 'Entertainment Airline' with a distinguished and unique coloring and image. Our passengers are all touched by the unusually cheerful attitude of our receptionists, which sets them apart from ordinary receptionists. It's truly a 'service unusual', as the name of this book suggests!"

Mr. Patee Sarasin
Chief Executive Officer, Nok Air, Thailand

"We create innovative concepts, dare to be different, and do what other companies do not dare to do. At DTAC, our service comes from the 'unusual hearts' of all our staff. This is exactly what George exhorts us to do in his book *Service Unusual* - stand out by going beyond the obvious!"

Mr. Vichai Bencharongkul
Chief Executive Officer, Total Access Communication Public Company Limited, Thailand

Acknowledgements

No man's an island. This book is an effort that can be attributed to numerous people in my life.

First of all, to my family and loved ones who never fail to believe in me: my parents and sisters. Thanks for allowing me to be myself.

To all colleagues whom I had the privilege to work with in various organisations. As the saying goes, "Iron sharpens iron." They have sharpened me with their care, support, encouragement and criticism. Especially my comrades in DistincTions Asia from Singapore, Hong Kong and Thailand who are living out our mission of helping to stretch people's potential every day.

And to everyone else who has touched my life in any way throughout my life journey thus far. You know who you are.

Last and most importantly, to my partner and comrade in life, my wife Chia Ly. You make me whole.

Contents

Introduction

"The service we render to others is really the rent we pay for our room on this earth. It is obvious that man is himself a traveller, that the purpose of this world is not 'to have and to hold' but 'to give and serve'. There can be no other meaning."

SIR WILFRED T. GRENFELL

Taming a Wild Horse

I learnt what true service is when I was in my mid 20s. I had just left a promising job in an international consulting firm to join ServiceMaster, a Fortune 500 company providing support management services to hospitals, schools, and factories. I was a trainee manager. The company believed in hands-on and grounds-up training. As part of my orientation, I was assigned to a major public hospital to learn and do housekeeping for two weeks.

The work was tough. I didn't enjoy it but I could take the physical demands. I went about my duties uneventfully for about a week. Then one day, my life was turned upside down. I was mopping a ward corridor when a group of doctors, on their daily round, made their way in my direction. As they approached, I heard a yell: "George!" I looked up from the vinyl floor and there he was, my classmate from high school. He was one of the doctors in the group. He looked like he had just seen a corpse. "George, WHAT are you doing here?"

I could not recall my response. All I remember was when I went home that night, I actually broke down and cried. I could take dirty toilets and inconsiderate visitors trampling on the floor I had just mopped. But to be a cleaner in front of my peers, the embarrassment and humiliation was just too much to bear. Like a true Asian, the loss of face was more than I could take.

The next morning, I threw down my resignation letter on my American General Manager's desk. He was calm. He had probably seen similar cases many times over. He patiently probed me for my reasons. After about 15 minutes, he took a deep breath, looked me straight in the eye and asked: "Do you know how a wild horse is tamed?"

The question took me by surprise. What did wild horses have to do with how I was feeling at that time? I shook my head in puzzlement.

"Well, I have seen enough John Wayne movies to tell you that to tame a wild horse, you need to ride it till its spirit is broken. Only then will it submit to you." He smiled.

I kept my silence.

He continued: "Your spirit was broken yesterday."

"My spirit?"

He smiled again. "Your spirit of pride. You see, service is a calling. It requires a spirit of humility and servanthood. Until you break your spirit of self and ego, you cannot submit yourself to truly serve others."

I mustered up the courage to rebut: "But what has cleaning floors got to do with my job as a manager?"

He was just waiting for this moment. "It has got to do with putting yourself in the shoes of the housekeepers who will be working for you. How can you manage them well if you do not bring yourself down to understand and feel what they go through?"

I could not claim that I understood the message conveyed to me that day. But I decided not to quit. Somehow, deep inside me, I was struck by his words. I was curious about my spirit of pride and humility. I wanted to hang around to find out.

Find out I did. I spent my formative professional years in the organisation. I became a Servant Leader (more about this in Chapter 9), a professional proud to serve others. I rose to become the country manager. My spirit of pride was broken. In its place is a spirit of service.

You may think: "This sounds touching. Very altruistic." Well, sorry. ServiceMaster is not in the charity business. One of its corporate objectives is "To Grow Profitably". This spirit of service is actually ServiceMaster's secret weapon. It distinguishes the company from its competitors and increases its value in the eyes of its customers. The spirit of service allows the New York Stock Exchange listed company to be profitable. My point here is that profit and service do come as a package.

Need to Understand Service

More than 70 per cent of new jobs today are in service-related industries. Everybody serves somebody. That somebody can be your customer, boss, colleague, even subordinate. Service is serious business indeed. Yet, how many of us truly understand service? How many of us have gotten our 'spirits broken' and been freed up to serve?

But there is already a slew of existing books teaching us what and how to serve. Many people follow what these books prescribe: across-the-board standards on service, behaviour, performance, etc. As a result, service has become indistinguishable and generic over time, a "Me Too" syndrome.

Herein lies the primary premise of this book. It sets out to look at service from a different perspective. It intentionally departs from conventional approaches to service. The rationale for doing so is simple: To stand out in this service economy where everyone is chasing and copying one another, we need to be different by going beyond the obvious. What is obvious becomes ordinary. Thus, to be successful in service and in life, we need to be unconventional and unusual.

The approach to this book is to highlight a series of commonly known and accepted service practices (I call them Service Usual Practices) and contrast them individually with corresponding service practices that might be known but not widely applied (conversely labelled as Service Unusual Practices).

Service is both an art and science. Ultimately, it is about providing an experience to the recipient. Certain key components need to be present in order for service to be excellent. The book introduces the

Service Experience Pyramid that is a framework of essential service components: Customers, Service Strategy, People, Process, Product, Leadership/Culture, and Measurements. Each component will be explored from a "reverse", non-ordinary angle.

This book is meant for practising managers and leaders whose work and purpose involve serving others. They are on a constant lookout to excel and distinguish themselves and their people. This book contains insights that will hopefully inspire readers to implement changes so that their services that will be relevant for the future.

Examples of service companies that successfully apply the Service Unusual practices are found throughout the book. Most books on service are written from a Western perspective. Thus I have intentionally included examples of Asian companies to illustrate the point that best service practices can originate in Asia.

I am also mindful that a book, rich in concepts but poor in application, is like a Ferrari without an engine. Appealing but useless. Therefore I have included a section called Personal Practice Tips at the end of each chapter. This section lists a series of possible applications of the contents from the chapter. In doing so, it also doubles up as a supplementary section.

Lastly, it is my ultimate wish that the insights and practices in this book will turn from "unusual" to "usual" very quickly. When that day comes, this book will be redundant. Then it is time for a sequel. Help me make it happen soon!

George T.K. Quek

GOING BEYOND HERD MENTALITY

*"Do not go where the path may lead,
go instead where there is no path and leave a trail."*

RALPH WALDO EMERSON
(1803-1882)

We all want to be different. To be unique and stand out.

Yet the reality is that we hardly practice what we preach. Instead, we are devout followers of the "Herd Mentality". We prefer to move together in a group, like herds of sheep. We better not stray. It is safer and less risky to stay together.

This mentality explains why we chase fads. Many people already have the latest fashion, mobile phones, and cars. Don't be left out!

This also explains why we show little tolerance for people who look and act differently from us. We show disdain for people who adopt unconventional lifestyles. We wonder why some of our fellow men decide to give up a six-figure salary to do social and missionary work. It is almost taboo to break an accepted norm.

For example, at the back of most of our minds, we see tertiary formal education as the key that opens the doors to success. But billionaires like Microsoft's Bill Gates, who became the richest man on earth, and Sim Wong Hoo, the Singaporean founder of Creative Technologies, the leading sound card maker in the world, share common experiences. Gates dropped out of Harvard University. Sim does not have a university degree. Both Gates and Sim took the road less travelled (by herds of sheep).

In the service industry today, we experience similar service treatments. Everyone seems to be pushing service to be faster, friendlier, more convenient etc. While this trend is good for us as customers, it cancels out our hard work as service providers. We become part of a herd of providers who look and act the same. Our customers cannot tell us apart.

We then think of new ways to stand out and be different to our customers. Meanwhile, our competitors are watching and following us. One such example is 3G mobile technology. Because telecommunication companies do not want to lose out to each other, when one came out with the service, others followed. The herd of sheep keeps going round and round and round and…But few, if any, have yet to make a cent from this.

This leads us to our first Service Unusual Practice:

Service Usual Practice #1:
We need to relentlessly spot and keep up with best customer practices to stay relevant.

Service Unusual Practice #1:
Stop benchmarking against others and become a benchmark for others.

Profit for Going Beyond the Obvious

I used to work for a successful entrepreneur who once advised me: "There is only profit for those who look and go beyond the obvious." I did not quite understand him at that time. Now that I am older and hopefully, wiser, I consider this advice as having enlightened my work and life.

Think about it. What is obvious to you is obvious to most of us as well. For the last 20 years, everyone is touting China as the market to be in. You probably conclude that you need to enter the Chinese market now or live to regret it. However, this is also obvious to many others. If I am given a dollar every time I hear this analysis, I will be wealthy beyond measure! Unfortunately, your opinions and decisions would be common and undifferentiating.

The Counter-Intuitive Latecomer

On the other hand, I know of a successful businessman who took an opposing view. He refused to enter the Chinese market in spite of advice from many of his peers to do so. He knew of many foreign investors who had gone into the market for a number of years and had yet to smell a single cent of return. They had spent much time learning and understanding the local market. In other words, they were first-movers who took a more long-term view.

The businessman did not have the deep pockets to rush in and hang on. His friends told him that this was regrettable because by the time he was ready to enter the market, he would be too late. He did not think so. As far as he could see, the Chinese market was still immature. Copyrights and intellectual property rights remained unprotected.

In July 2004, the Chinese authorities overturned the patent rights of pharmaceutical giant Pfizer's erectile-dysfunctional drug, Viagra, making it possible for local competitors to use the ingredients. Many first-movers had local partners who, after learning and copying their products and knowledge, set up competing entities. The businessman believed that it was never too late. Let the competiton fight it out. Once the dust settled and competitors weakened from the fight, he would move in with newer and better products. The Chinese consumers would become more mature and informed over time. They would appreciate and accept alternatives. Brand loyalty is no longer a given.

Today, this entrepreneur is smoking his favourite Cuban cigar at the Grand Hyatt atop the Jin Mao Tower in Shanghai, celebrating another year of double-digit percentage growth. In between puffs, he sips his Dom Perignon and thanks his competitors for paving the way for him.

Well, he is just lucky, you think. The bottom-line is that his counter-intuitive judgement paid off!

Challenging the "Levelling" Effect

Our world is constantly "levelling". Few persons, products and services can stand out for long before competition neutralises their edge. It is difficult to be truly unique today. For example, mobile phone service providers in Thailand have lowered their prices drastically to grow their customer bases in a fast maturing market. Consumers used to consider the providers' service levels and quality of coverage. But price competition has forced the providers to keep up with one another such that it is increasingly difficult to differentiate their quality and offerings.

Using price cuts to attract and keep customers is not sustainable in the long run. In Singapore, when bubble tea was still a craze, many entrepreneurs jumped on the bandwagon to retail the drink. A price war ensued and eventually many shops closed down as the craze died.

This levelling effect makes it more imperative for us to be different. To do this, we must avoid the herd mentality, this is, to want to follow the masses. We should learn not to readily accept conventions and traditions. Sometimes we need to swim against the tide, and we may not be right all the time. Many traditions are good and worthy. Yet, breakthroughs come about when we question norms and act against them. Let's look at how Michael Dell did it.

Taking On the Giants

Michael S. Dell was born in Houston, Texas, in 1965. He attended my alma mater, the University of Texas at Austin, intending to be a doctor. Instead, he started a computer business in his dormitory room in 1984 with merely US$1,000.

He questioned the conventional costs and methods of retailing computers. He was driven by an unprecedented idea to build relationships directly with customers. At that time, to buy a computer, you would need to walk into a retail store. If you decided to purchase it, you would either need to lug the computer back home and install it yourself, or you could pay a little more and wait for at least a few days for the computer to be delivered to your home.

Dell saw computers as a commodity. He betted that the differentiator in this business would be the selling method. So he dropped out of university at age 19 and started selling his own brand directly to the customers via phone and later, the internet. This method eliminates the costly retail middleman and allows for more efficient solutions.

The company focuses on keeping costs down and passing them onto the customers. It maintains no finished-goods inventories, practically no component inventories, building only to order, and selling and delivering the completed PC units direct to customers.

By doing so, he went against the "Goliaths" of the industry like Compaq and IBM that had more powerful brand recognition. These giants would later concede by setting up direct selling channels to keep up with Dell.

And the result of going beyond the obvious? Today, Michael Dell is the richest person under the age of 40. Dell Inc. is the 93rd largest company in the world as of 2003 (Fortune) with revenue exceeding US$45 billion. To top it off, Dell Inc. is the most profitable PC manufacturer in the world with more than 50,000 employees around the globe.

We all love success stories like Dell's. They inspire us. But does it stop right here? Are we going to act on the learning points for our own lives?

Well, Michael Dell said: "It's through curiosity and looking at opportunities in new ways that we've always mapped our path at Dell. There's always an opportunity to make a difference."

The Rise of the Service Industry

I have worked in the service industry throughout my professional career. I am part of the rule, not the exception, as more than 70 per cent of us are doing service work today.

Unless you have been in a coma for the last 50 years, you would realise we live in a service economy. We wake up to a McDonald's breakfast, take the public transport to work, chat with friends via a mobile network, liaise with the company's lawyers, have lunch at a local restaurant, visit the family dentist for the annual check-up, deposit cash at the nearest bank branch, shop and eat in the mall after work, and unwind at a popular watering hole before going to bed.

The line between products and services is increasingly blurred. Both offer customers benefits. *But with a product, you are offering the customer the promise of benefits. The customer has to use the product to derive the benefits. With service, the service provider is responsible for delivering the benefits directly to the customer.*

Customers today expect their needs to be met in a holistic manner. This "bundled and packaged" approach of products and services is common everywhere. Dell saw this. With increasing commoditisation of products, businesses are realising the power of service as a competitive differentiator. When you buy a car, you are not just getting a product used for travelling. Your buying decision will determine how convenient it is to obtain the optimal car loan and insurance, as well as how comfortable your driving trip can be in the form of the leather seats and accessories like television and GPS. When your car is due for servicing, your decision will be determined by how fast and hassle-free the maintenance service is. All these are services relating to the car product.

In the Organisation for Economic Co-operation and Development (OECD), which includes the developed economies of the world like the United States and the European Union, manufacturing has slipped to less than 20 per cent of its GDP, while conversely, service has risen to more than 70 per cent.

Service is everywhere! It is like water or air: we cannot do without them yet we will not truly appreciate them until they disappear or turn bad. We hear more complaints than compliments from customers. When we receive satisfactory service, we take it for granted. This is what we pay for and expect. When service goes wrong, we raise our heckles and voices.

Are We Ready for the Service Economy?

We are contradictory creatures. We constantly lament the poor state of service to anyone who cares to hear. But many of us are performing these very services. This begs the question: Are we ready for the service economy?

The answer lies in the way we look at service. Most of us see service work as inferior. Service is perceived as lowly servitude. I once proposed to give a talk entitled "Servant Leadership" touching on key leadership principles to the management team of a leading telecommunications company in Hong Kong. They agreed that leaders serve but insisted that I changed the title of the talk. When I asked why, they sheepishly told me that the word "servant" was degrading.

In our Asian culture, where class is highly valued, people who serve are placed at the bottom of the hierarchy.

Unconvinced? Just ask any young person what he or she would like to do. The answers come fast: Doctor, Lawyer, Software Engineer, Designer, Entertainer and Banker. These are all service professions. Next, you ask the same young person why he or she chooses the profession. This time round, you will sense a slight pause before receiving an altruistic but unconvincing: "Well, I want to use my skills to give back to society." You are cynical so you dig deeper before you learn the real reason: Respect, Glamour, Wealth, and Status etc. You get the point.

To think unconventionally in the service industry means we need to look at services from a positive light. We must see it as a profession in its own right. We must work towards the day when we are all proud to be called service professionals. Most importantly, we need to instil this professionalism and pride in our service workers. They need to be better treated, paid and developed.

Personal Practice Tips:

- Accept the reality that serving others is a noble calling. Service is not degrading.

- Make it a discipline to be inquisitive. Do not accept information and situations at face value.

- Always ask "Why?" to ascertain the root cause or reason of any matter. Practice thinking about reasons and logic behind current affairs when reading the newspaper.

- Then go a step further by asking "What else?" or "What is really happening?"

- Dare to take counter-intuitive risks after consideration.

- Always adopt a "contingency" mindset. Do not sit still.

Chapter

2

DISCOVERING THE SERVICE EXPERIENCE PYRAMID

"Customer Experience – Own it!"

DELL'S SLOGAN

In their landmark book, *The Experience Economy,* authors B. Joseph Pines II and James H. Gilmore state that in order to go beyond the obvious, many companies are moving beyond services and solutions into experiences. Thus McDonald's offers more than a meal. It will host your child's birthday party, complete with a candle-lit cake, party host and entertainment. Walt Disney, with their Disney Parks, is the recognised expert in offering experiences. Walt Disney sees its customers as guests who are there to be happy.

Pines and Gilmore believe that experiences are a distinct offering from services. Experiences provide a memorable offering that will remain with us for a long time. To achieve this, we must be drawn to feel a sensation using all 5 senses. And to feel the sensation, we require highly skilled service providers who can dynamically personalise each service transaction according to our needs, responses and behavioural traits.

Ritz Carlton hotels, for example, are famed for gathering and remembering customer preferences. A friend of mine who is a frequent traveller, stayed in a Ritz Carlton hotel in an Asian city where he indicated his preference for apple juice. A couple of years later, when he checked in at a Ritz Carlton in the US, he was surprised to see that the mini-bar in his room was filled with cans of apple juice.

Sir Colin Marshall, the former British Airways chairman, said: *"What British Airways does is to go beyond the function and compete on the basis of providing an experience."* The aircraft and the flight is the setting, for a distinctive en route experience.

Service Usual Practice #2:
World-class service goes beyond satisfying customers' needs to providing solutions for them.

Service **Unusual** Practice #2:
World-class service goes beyond providing solutions, to ensure that the customer has a memorable experience being served.

What is a Service Experience?

Whenever I check in at my regular hotel in Hong Kong, the receptionist will greet me with a mechanical "Good afternoon, Welcome". Before I have time to respond, the check-in process is over and my room key is given to me. All I need to do is to sign on the check-in form and hand over my credit card. All my particulars and preferences would already be captured in the hotel's check-in computer system. Without fail, I would be given a non-smoking room with a king-size bed on a high floor.

Sometimes, I will attempt to make small talk with the receptionist. "So who is performing at the lounge?"

"You can ask the concierge. Have a good stay. Next please!"

Contrast this experience with the one in Bangkok. Upon alighting from the taxi, the doorman at my regular hotel would call out my name and rush to help me with my bags. Later, the well-groomed receptionist would give me a smile so warm it could melt an iceberg. I would then be kindly requested to fill in the check-in form.

"Sorry, Mr. Quek, could you also write down your home address and passport number?"

"But this is like my thirtieth stay! Shouldn't you have the information already?"

"Sorry, sir," she smiled apologetically and showed off more of her pearly whites.

When I entered my room, I found that the bed was not king-sized.

"Sorry, Mr. Quek. We are full today. Please call us to change the room for you tomorrow."

"But I made the room reservation more than a month ago!"

"Sorry, sir." I could almost feel her smile through the phone.

The hotel in Hong Kong was very efficient and even effective in giving me what I wanted. But I felt like one of the hundreds of guests being herded through the system. There was no personal touch. The process was up to par but the people were not.

On the other hand, I found plenty of personal warmth in the hotel in

Bangkok. Yet, I could not get what I wanted. The people were up to par but the process was not.

My experience in the different hotels involved both:
• Tangibles – a non-smoking room with a king-sized bed on a high floor.
• Intangibles – the soft and emotional aspects to service like courteous, knowledgeable staff.

An experience comprises tangible and intangible factors. They include products, processes and people. Customers today are demanding a *Service Experience that consists of all possible customer contact points throughout the entire service delivery process.* These contact points must be consistent and manage to exceed the customer's needs. They combine to satisfy the customer in all 5 senses of taste, sight, touch, smell and sound.

Intangibles differentiate an experience from a solution. Solutions are bundled services to meet the customer's multiple but related needs. A photocopier shop will not only make copies of your documents. It has extended its services to help design the layout of your documents as well as to deliver the finished copies to your desired destination. But to give you an experience, the copies would arrive in attractive carton boxes with a seal across each box stating "Quality copies from XXX company" giving you the assurance of reliability and quality. Better yet, the executive from the photocopying company will call and ask if everything is in order, connoting care and concern.

Airlines used to compete on who can provide the best cabin service experience: gourmet cuisine (taste), attractive and attentive attendants (sight and feel), comfortable full reclining leather seats (touch), choices of entertainment and music (sight and sound) and even designer toiletries (smell). This cabin experience is now levelled. Any full-service airline that does not match its competitors cannot expect to survive on its own.

Airlines now realise that their customer experience and contact with them are not confined to the flight itself. Instead it begins from the moment the prospective customer decides to book a ticket and continues to post-flight activities like baggage handling. Thus the next competitive arena involves Internet ticket purchase, advance seat allocation, pre-flight and in-town check-ins, limousine service to the airport, luxurious passenger lounges as well as faster baggage handling.

Once a service organisation is awakened to the concept of service experience, their scope of customer service is enlarged and enhanced.

Service Experience is Profitable!

Commodities	Products	Services	Experience
Coffee Beans	Nescafé Instant Coffee Mix	McDonald's	Starbucks

US$0.18 ⟶ US$2.25

Theodore Levitt devised the Total Product Concept in which every offering has 4 levels of incarnations:

1. Generic: The fundamental, but rudimentary, substantive product service like coffee beans. This is analogous with commodities.

2. Expected: Adds to the generic all the traditional services

customers expect, like processing coffee beans. This is analogous with instant coffee mix.

3. Augmented: Adds to the expected a bundle of benefits the customers do not expect, like ready hot coffee to be served. This is analogous with a coffee served at outlets.

4. Potential: Adds to the augmented latent benefits that even the customers are not aware of like having a choice of coffee in a comfortable and hip environment. No detail is left to chance. All 5 senses are managed: the choice of music, smell, lighting, room temperature, ample choices of coffee. All these are carefully aligned to be consistent with the "coffee" experience Starbuck is providing.

Customers are willing to pay an increasingly large premium for the extra value represented by each succeeding level. Starbucks is able to charge US$2.25 for a cup of coffee that actually costs US$0.18 per kilogramme of beans. That's value-add at its best!

Holistic and Integrated Approach to Service

The service experience is more than just a smile or greeting. Neither is it just a systematic process.

Service is both an art and a science. It requires a holistic and comprehensive approach that considers components like Customers, Strategy, Leadership/Culture, People, Processes and Service Measures. All components must be aligned to bring about the desired customer experience. The various components are depicted in the form of a pyramid:

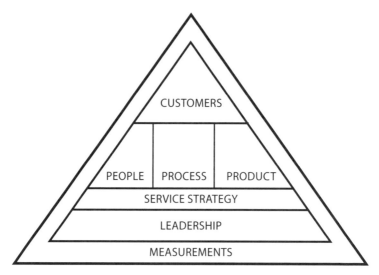

The Service Experience Pyramid

The Service Experience Pyramid

Customers rightfully occupy the apex of the pyramid, as they are the recipients of the benefits from service experience. They are our paymasters and they determine if the service is of value. We will look at how to intimately understand our customers in Chapter 3. In addition, we will explore how our customers think about and value our services in Chapter 4.

The 3 Ps: People, Process and Product combine to produce the intended service experience for the customer. The people factor will be covered in Chapter 6, after which we will take a look at the importance of Process/Product in the delivery of service in Chapter 7.

The service strategy forms the plan or roadmap for the 3Ps that serve as the means. We will be looking at how strategies can be streamlined to cater to target audiences in Chapter 5.

The management of service performance is achieved through the establishment of appropriate measures that help actualise and monitor every component of the pyramid to ensure the attainment of service goals. That is why measurements border the entire pyramid. What cannot be measured cannot be managed. In Chapter 8, we will take a look at how proper measurements can be done.

Leadership, on the other hand, is at the bottom rung of the pyramid. This does not mean this component is the least important. Instead, Leadership forms the foundation of the entire service chain. It determines the strategy that formulates the way people, processes and products work together to provide the customers with the expected service experience. Leadership will be dealt with in Chapter 9.

Through the subsequent chapters, we will look at each component differently and more discerningly from most.

Personal Practice Tips:

- Do you still see yourself offering stand-alone services or products? If so, integrate all your offerings to include both products and services to provide an experience.

- Pay attention to all customer contact points, especially the pre and post-purchase stages.

- Put yourself in the shoes of the customer and take yourself through the service experience of your operations. What does your customer experience at every possible contact point with you?

- Note areas where your services are inconsistent or lacking. For example, having friendly phone operators but keeping the caller on hold for a long time. Consider both tangible and intangible, process and people factors.

- Check your service experiences against the 5 senses of sight, hearing, smell, taste and feel. You can serve the best noodles in your eatery but make sure your toilet is clean and the air-conditioning is working well. The key is consistency.

- Remember, your customers come to you to meet their emotional needs. Is your service experience able to make them "feel good"?

SENSING OUR CUSTOMERS

"Customer is GOD."

COMMON SAYING IN CHINA

There is no greater accolade than to be called a "God". Customers are our lifeline and the reason why we exist.

This chapter and the following two look into the planning and marketing aspects of service experience. Everything starts with the customer.

When our customers tell us to jump, we ask "How High?" To stay in their good books, we have to know how to please them and pander to their every wish. We must understand them so intimately that we can anticipate their need even before they realise it.

Furthermore, try to imagine how dehumanising it is, when we call our favourite bank, only to hear the response: "What is your account number?" The so-called "God" is reduced to a series of digits. A basic premise of providing a service experience is the ability to personalise the experience for the customer. Instead of just being a digit, customers want to be known by their names, preferences, etc.

We are close to paranoid about what our customers think of us. If the "God" is happy with us, we will be blessed. If not, hell knows no greater fury. That is why we are constantly asking them to rate us. "On a scale of 1 to 10, how satisfied are you with our services?" We happily report to our boss that "96.3% of our customers rate us above average last quarter". We therefore deserve more rewards because our "God" is happy. Correction: "God" *was* happy. The same 96.3% was happy last quarter but might not be today.

Our customers want an on-going relationship with us. They are the recipients of the service experience we provide. We therefore need to know what they want to experience. To do that, we have to be their constant confidants. To talk with and listen to them regularly. They want us to partner them to meet their changing needs. They hope that we can faithfully hear and empathise with their problems and concerns, and then come up with answers for them.

Service Usual Practice #3:

To be able to provide a customer experience, we have to faithfully track the level of our customer satisfaction to determine how well we are doing.

Service Unusual Practice #3:

Kick the habit of relying just on customer ratings. If we really want to know our customers, ask and listen for their qualitative feedback.

Addicted to Numbers

Jack Welch, the former Chairman and CEO of General Electric, said it all: "Numbers aren't the vision. Numbers are the product. I never talk about numbers."

Customer satisfaction survey is now an integral part of most service operations. No decent service organisation will admit that it does not consciously gather input and feedback from its customers. The intent is sound. To serve customers, we need to understand what they need and want.

But our customers are living, breathing beings. They are not numbers. When we look at most customer feedback exercises, the bulk of what is asked is quantitative. Customers are asked to give numerical or categorical ratings for various aspects of service received. Then, almost as a symbolic gesture, the last few questions allow the customers to voice their views and opinions of the service received and/or the organisation.

Just visit any restaurant or hotel chain. Conveniently placed at each table or room is a snazzy customer feedback card (forms are considered too lengthy). Often, to encourage more customers to fill up the feedback cards, organisations offer incentives. I was travelling on a major Asian airline carrier when I was invited to fill in a lengthy customer survey. Along with the form, I was given a gift pack for my efforts. On top of that, the survey form entitled me to a lucky draw for free air tickets.

Why do organisations rely so much on quantitative feedback?

Well, we are more comfortable with numbers. Ratings and percentages are measurable and comparative. Bosses depend on numbers to judge us on results. Numbers are an objective way to let us know how well or badly we are doing serving our customers. If the number of customers who rate us "Above Average" increases by 5 per cent compared to last year, we must be doing something right.

One problem with quantitative feedback is they tend to be retrospective. The numbers tell us no more than how well we are perceived by our customers for our past performance. They do not indicate what we should do for the future other than improving on areas of operations indicated by poor numbers.

Compare numbers with qualitative comments like "They have done a great job!" or "The service is slow". Though qualitative feedback also tells us how we are doing, it is difficult to summarise for bosses to gauge our overall performance.

Qualitative Inputs are More Revealing

Assess the following feedback:

"Responsiveness of Service is rated at 85%", "The percentage of queries that were resolved on the first call has gone up by 24% over the last quarter"

And

"Service is slow during lunch hours", "I was put on hold thrice and had to speak to four different hotline operators before I got the answer I wanted"

If we want to improve our services, which feedback is more useful? Service is never totally objective. What is fast? What is personable?

You and I probably have different expectations. Quantifiable feedback attempts to force qualitative expectations into a readable form for us to make business and management decisions, much like trying to squeeze a square peg into a round hole.

Qualitative customer inputs are more valuable. Let's take the above analogy as an example. Management can pat themselves on their backs when they are told that 24% more customer calls were satisfactorily handled on the first attempt. The call centre staff are handed performance bonuses.

If we want to look beyond the obvious, pay more attention to what the customer is saying: "Yes, you did manage to resolve my problem on my first call, but my experience with this one call was tedious and stressful. Your call centre staff could not address my problem. They had to pass my call around to 4 different persons until the manager herself took my call and addressed my concern. In the process, I was kept on hold three times and I had to repeat my query because I was put to three different people. So frustrating! I wish these call centre people are better trained to handle different situations."

Qualitative inputs can point us to the root causes of service issues. In this example, knowledge, or the lack of it is the issue. Such inputs can also give us invaluable insights on how to improve our services and create new products and solutions for our markets.

"Super Size Me!"

Recently McDonald's abolished the long-standing "Super Size" practice in which customers are encouraged to pay a little more for a bigger serving of fries and drinks. Consumers who are concerned about the health impact of too much fast food prompted the decision.

There was even a movie made by American Morgan Spurlock named *Supersize Me!* in which Spurlock documented himself eating nothing but McDonald's food for an entire month. At the end of it, he put on 12 kilogrammes and had chronic liver problems. This documentary epitomised the already strong social aversions against fast food in general. As a result of such strong customer reactions, McDonald's has responded by upgrading its menus in various countries to include healthier items like sandwiches and yogurts.

Gary Hamel, a leading strategy expert and author of *Competing for the Future,* summed it up nicely: "Being customer-led is not good enough. You need to get to your customers deep, unarticulated needs."

If qualitative customer feedback is key, then the next practice should get your attention.

Service Usual Practice #4:
Customer complaints indicate that we are lacking. Therefore our goal is to minimise and avoid complaints.

Service Unusual Practice #4:
Customer complaints are useful. We should encourage our customers to complain more.

Love Complaints!

We don't generally like complaints. They represent faults on our part or criticisms from our customers. They are negative. They get us into trouble with our bosses. They stress us out when we have to resolve them. They embarrass and belittle us when the unhappy customers scream in our faces.

No wonder a complaint is like bitter medication. Both are not well liked. But seriously, there is no better form of direct, honest and heart-felt customer feedback than a good complaint.

Good complaint? A good complaint is a valid one in which the customer has a genuine cause to be unhappy about the service received. A submitted application form that got lost. The repairman who came two hours late after repeated assurances that he would be on time. Much can be learnt from these complaints.

Of course, there are unwarranted complaints. Customers can be unreasonable and irrational at times. When told in advance to expect a processing lead-time of two weeks, a credit card applicant wrote to complain about the wait only after a week. A waiter, who accidentally spilt water on a patron, immediately apologised and used a hair-dryer to dry the shirt; and yet he received a complaint letter.

But even these complaints can give us tips for improvement. The credit card company worked to shorten its application process to about a week because they received similar complaints, prompted by the fact that their competitors were able to approve credit cards faster. Today, credit cards are pre-approved. Customer demands and competition pressure forced the changes.

All complaints are valuable customer inputs. We need to welcome them like a VIP visiting our homes. But we don't go all out just to create complaints. That will be disastrous. Complaints will come naturally. Why? Because we are never perfect. Because we are in a constant struggle to keep up and exceed changing customer expectations.

Does that mean the more complaints the merrier? We still want to minimise complaints. Too many complaints, especially of the same nature, are a flashlight warning signal that we are taking our customers for granted. The bottom-line is while we work towards minimising complaints, we welcome them and perceive them as valuable.

The "Complaint is Good" Mindset

Service organisations need to adopt a "complaint is good" attitude. We have to move away from being defensive about criticisms. Instead, we need to develop "thicker skins" and welcome complaints.

World-class organisations do not wait for complaints to come. They go look for them. Back to Jack Welch. He made it a point of personally meeting GE's major customers in the spring and fall of every year. He credited much of his and GE's customer insights to these reality checks with customers. John Chambers, CEO of Cisco Systems, spends a substantial amount of his time with customers. He expects his senior managers to do the same.

It is common to see organisations calling customers soon after the service to seek views and opinions on the received service. Recently, a week after I had sent my car to a Shell Pro-Serve centre for regular servicing, I got a call from a customer service representative from the Shell main office asking me about my service experience. It was obvious that the representative was more interested in getting my opinions on how else the service can be improved than merely probing me to give the service a rating.

Unfortunately, many service providers have played "hide-and-seek" with customers before. How many times did you demand to see the manager but was told he was busy or not around? When you insisted, the staff promised to get the manager to call you later. This is a good strategy. It allows you time to cool off and calm down. But instead you got more agitated because that call never came.

Front-line staff constitutes a crucial feedback channel. They are the contact points with the customers. Unfortunately, many of them do not go out of their way to obtain feedback because doing so is like shooting themselves in the foot. "If the customer complains, I have to account for it." It does not help that many complaints are about them.

We need a *"no blame"* mindset here. We have to convince our front-line staff that a complaint is primarily for improvement and not finger pointing. It is a wake-up call. The message to our staff is: "It is ok to make mistakes. Just do not repeat them. Because if you do, you are not learning from them." Over time, our staff will see complaints as a means to learn and improve. That is what a complaint should be good for! In other words, complaints should be seen as blaming the sin, not the sinner.

We can go one step further and actually formalise quantity of customer feedback as a performance measure for the front-line staff. If the target is met, incentives are handed out to them. I used to run a logistic business. I set up an incentive scheme for the couriers based on the number of feedback cards they had solicited from their customers. It did not matter if the feedback was positive or not. We just wanted our customers to speak up!

Listening Posts

There are several ways we can obtain feedback, but basically we have to make it easy and convenient for customers to talk to us. To do so, we need to open up more channels of communication with our customers. Commonly used channels are phone feedback forms, hotlines and e-mails. In Singapore, many government bodies appoint full-time Quality Service Managers who are directly contactable by the public.

On the next page is a table listing some common methods of gathering qualitative customer inputs. We had earlier touched on the use of complaints, the importance of front-line staff as our ears, as well as the need for direct management contacts with customers.

In addition, other common information gathering methods include conducting customer focus-groups to hear customers out and getting independent parties to act as mystery shoppers to get first-hand accounts of the service experience.

All these listening initiatives actually represent part of our customers' experience with us. By demonstrating that we are open to listening to their opinions and desires, we leave with them the impression that we care and take them seriously.

One consulting firm listens using the 80/20 rule. It concentrates on studying their top key clients' present and future needs, their challenges and opportunities with the objective of generating customised solutions to these clients' needs and challenges. These are people who will make up the bulk of its income.

So far, we have been focusing on our existing customers. A powerful yet under-utilised means is talking to customers who have left or not been buying from us for quite a while. They can reveal why they are not doing business with us. More importantly, they can tell us why they are buying from our competitors instead.

MODE	Use of Complaints	Listen to Front-Line Staff	Direct Management Contacts	Lost and Absentee Customer interviews	Key client studies	Customer Panels (Focus Groups)	Transaction-based studies (Mystery Shopping)
COST	Low	Low	Low	Moderate	Moderate	Moderate to High	Moderate to High
TIME	Low	Low	Low	Moderate	Moderate	Moderate to High	Moderate to High
MAIN USES	Identify problems in the service process	Find out details on execution of customer touch-points	Find out details on execution of customer touch-points	Find out service defects as well as how the competitors fare.	In-depth information on most important customers	Continuous source of information on changing customers' expectations	Provides first-hand feedback on performance of each component of Service Quality. Good for tracking performance of front-line staff.

Table 4.1 Different ways to obtain customers inputs

Quantifying the Qualitative

Hopefully you are now convinced that qualitative feedback is vital. But where does this leave our quantitative feedback?

They are still useful in pointing out service performance gaps. They are useful for reporting and measuring purposes.

Again, if we go beyond the obvious, we would ask: "Must quantitative and qualitative feedback be mutually exclusive?"

We know both forms of feedback serve their purposes. But why can't we quantify qualitative information for reporting and measuring purposes? We can. One common form of doing so is to categorise the qualitative comments. For example, I have worked with an exhibition and conference centre to analyse its written complaints and compliments. Feedback is grouped by services:

Feedback Categories	# of Complaints 1st Quarter	# of Complaints 2nd Quarter	# of Compliments 1st Quarter	# of Compliments 2nd Quarter
Events	15	12	3	2
Banquets	8	11	1	0
Conferences	2	1	4	3
Food & Beverage	25	18	9	8

In this way, quantity of complaints and compliments can be compared across time and categories of services. An increase in complaints can mean a drop in service levels. Of course, there could be other mitigating factors. Be wary of staff who suppress complaints or manipulate compliments so that the statistics look good.

Another categorisation is by service dimensions. We can group feedback according to aspects of service like speed, courtesy, environment etc. So you see, we can have the best of both worlds: We can benefit from more revealing qualitative feedback and still summarise them in an objective quantitative format to help us make management decisions!

Personal Practice Tips:

- Don't over-rely on customer satisfaction ratings. They can only tell you how you did in the past.

- Add more open-ended questions to your customer feedback form or survey to find out customers' future needs and wants.

- Spend at least 25 per cent of your time meeting and talking with your customers.

- Demand that your staff do the same, spending at least 1/3 of their time doing it.

- Do exit interviews with customers who want to discontinue doing business with you. Find out why they want to leave.

- Data-mine your customer list and determine the customers who have not been doing business for a while. Give them a courtesy call and find out why they have not been coming to you.

- Make customer feedback your top priority. No matter how busy you are, drop everything if a customer wants to complain.

- Reward staff for compliments received but do not punish people because of complaints. Constantly stress to everyone that complaints are meant for improvement. Only take punitive measures against those who keep repeating the same mistakes.

- Categorise complaints and compliments by types to analyse where your strengths and weaknesses are.

Chapter

4

SEEKING CUSTOMER VALUE

"Quality in a product or service is not what the supplier puts in.
It is what the customer gets out and is willing to pay for. A product is not
quality because it is hard to make and costs a lot of money,
as manufacturers typically believe. This is incompetence.
Customers pay only for what is of use to them and gives them value.
Nothing else constitutes quality."

PETER DRUCKER

Competition is forcing many of us to work hard to keep our customers. We realise that increasing market share is beating a dead horse. The next goldmine is customer share: that is, getting our existing customers to buy more. Great rewards await those of us who can keep our customers faithful and help them ward off the temptations of our competitors.

We shall delve deep to understand the factors behind customer loyalty. We will realise that customer loyalty is not what it is made out to be.

Service Usual Practice #5:

We know it is so much harder to win a new customer than it is to keep an existing one. Therefore we have to work hard to ensure that our customers are loyal to us.

Service **Unusual** Practice #5:

Customer Loyalty is Dead! Customers are only as loyal as the value they get from you.

Share of Customer's Pocket

"Levelling" and competition have changed the business landscape significantly. Over the last 50 years, the buzzword has been "market share". Businesses have perfected the art of acquiring customers. Proctor & Gamble proudly stated in its 2000 annual report that it sold more than 300 products to more than 5 billion people in 140 countries. Imagine that in our world of 6 billion or so people, P&G has already reached 5 out of 6 people. Where can P&G go from here? Our markets are maturing fast.

If market share has hit a wall, we can go around it and move on to "customer share". This is the art of Customer Loyalty: retaining existing customers and getting them to buy more from us. The telecommunications industry is facing market saturation everywhere. According to research company TNS, the average mobile phone penetration in Asia was 67 per cent in 2004 with rates going as high as 83 per cent in Hong Kong. DTAC, the second largest telecom company in Thailand, has admitted: "With growth rates slowing, it would become more important than ever to focus on controlling 'churn' (customer turnover)".

So everyone is scrambling to keep customers loyal, doing everything possible to maintain and increase the "share of the customer's pocket". But is customer loyalty worthy of being hailed as our next strategic rescuer?

Customer's "Love" is Conditional

I started a new business providing corporate training during the economic downturn of the early 2000s. Many people around me thought I was crazy. The world around me assumed that many businesses were not doing well. What chance would a new start-up like mine have?

I was merely applying **Service Unusual Practice #1: Stop benchmarking against others and become a benchmark for others.** I scanned beyond what the world was thinking. What I saw were many prospective customers who had become more cost-conscious during the sluggish economy. In the past when resources were in abundance, customers would not mind paying a little more to their regular suppliers and vendors who were safer and tested choices. But when times turned bad, they became more open to alternate offerings that could give better value for money. This represented an opportunity for competitors like me. My business was profitable within a year.

Many businesses hold up customer loyalty as a goal. They believe that if they continue to stay ahead of their customers' needs, they have nothing to worry about. This is true. *But the test of loyalty is when we cannot meet up to our customers' expectations.* When that happens, are your customers going to continue to stay with you?

If yes, congratulations! Customer loyalty is alive and well. Loyalty, in this context, is unconditional commitment between two persons or parties. Like in our personal lives, we talk about unconditional love. "Honey, I will always love you no matter what!"

But if your answer is no, then your customer loyalty rating is not going sky high.

Remember brands like Arthur Andersen and Pan-Am Airlines? In spite of the power of branding, we will eventually pay the penalty of extinction if we start to fall behind our customers' expectations.

So how loyal are your customers?

Customer Value

If customer loyalty is not what it is cut out to be, what is the new customer strategy?

Value is a simple concept. It is the difference between inputs and outputs. If the benefits we get out of an endeavour are more than the effort and resources we put in, we get positive value out of this endeavour. The reverse is also true: if output is less than input, we are stuck with negative value.

Similarly,

> Customer Value = Perceived Benefits – Perceived Costs

Perceived customer costs refer to the tangible and intangible costs from the customer's perspective. They include the price the customer pays to buy the service, as well as the effort needed by the customer to purchase, use and maintain the service. It is not all about money. A discount outlet selling branded clothes might offer good prices.

However, it is located far away from the city. There is no service staff on duty to help. The merchandise is thrown randomly in a pile. There is no return or exchange policy. You need to spend time getting to the store and then have to go through the hassle of rummaging through the merchandise to find something you like. Any piece of clothing you buy cannot be returned or exchanged after the sale transaction. All these are opportunity customer costs.

Perceived customer benefits, on the other hand, are the returns that the customer believes he/she has gained from the experience. Like costs, benefits too can be both tangible and intangible. Let's say you find a genuine Giorgio Armani woollen two-piece suit at the discount outlet at 50 per cent of the price you would need to pay at the Armani boutique downtown. You wear the suit to a sales pitch and so impress the prospect with your professionalism and grooming that you get the deal. That is a tangible benefit of buying the suit. In addition, owning and wearing an Armani suit makes you feel confident and cheerful. That's an intangible benefit!

Customer Value does not replace Customer Loyalty. Instead, *Customer Value explains Customer Loyalty.* As long as our customers continue to derive positive value in buying from us, they may stay loyal. Why may? It depends on what values our competitors are providing. Sustained loyalty only happens if our customer value is greater than our competitors'!

Therefore to retain our customers, we must continually ensure that the value of our services is always one step ahead of our competitors'. Given the trend of levelling discussed Chapter 1, our rivals are constantly on the move to match and exceed our customer value. Who says life is easy?

Many organisations mistakenly think that lowering prices alone will increase their customer value. We see too many victims of price competition. What they do not realise is that customer value is more than just price (customer cost). Price is only one side of the customer value's equation. Don't forget the other side of the coin: customer benefits. Patek Philippe watches are not cheap but they are perceived to be luxurious classic collectibles. Owners of these watches consider them worthwhile in spite of the high prices. Branding is a powerful customer benefit. The Apple's iPOD digital music player is more expensive than competing products that work better and have longer battery lives. Yet the iPOD is a best seller because it is considered an icon of technology, a symbol of "cool". Customers who are seen with iPODs are considered up-to-date and "in".

When we truly understand customer value, we realise that we have more tricks in our bag than pricing to compete with. I admit that in an intensely competitive market, price would be a factor but there are other differentiating factors. We might charge 10 per cent more than our nearest competitor but we offer more attentive service staff, faster delivery and longer warranty periods. Our customers do not mind paying a little more for lower intangible customer costs like more responsive service, and higher customer benefits like better warranty terms. In our customers' eyes, we provide better customer value than our cheaper competitor.

Bread Boutique

One company that capitalises on customer value is BreadTalk, a publicly listed company based in Singapore. It sells bread and confections. We cannot get more basic and conventional than that.

What BreadTalk sets out to do in order to create customer value is to

A BreadTalk store in Singapore (Courtesy of BreadTalk)

heighten the "glamour" of bread. They do so with practices such as:

- Creating visually appealing breads with a variety of stuffing and condiments that have catchy names like "Flosss", "Crouching Tiger, Hidden Bacon" and "Mount Fuji".

- Innovating and introducing new products regularly.

- Using the freshest and finest ingredients.

- Hand-making the products on-site to guarantee freshness.

- Adopting an open and "see-through" store concept, in which customers can purchase the products in a brightly lit environment utilising glass panels and sleek display shelves. Customers can actually see the production process that takes place behind the glass partition.

- "Professionalising" the bakers by putting them and their assistants in all-white chef outfits. BreadTalk likes to call them "Executive Chefs cum Designers"

BreadTalk sells their breads for around US$1 a piece. Not actually bargain basement prices but affordable. The growing number of people who flock to its outlets in Singapore, Malaysia, Indonesia, the Philippines, China, Taiwan and the Middle East, find value in BreadTalk's fresh and creative products sold in visually and olfactorily appealing surroundings (an experience!).

In 2004, BreadTalk was given a "Design for Asia" award by the Hong Kong Design Centre. Imagine that a bread maker winning accolades for design!

Service and Customer Value

Before we go on, it is important we discuss how service and customer value are linked. I am sure you have heard and read about different definitions of service. The most common one is "meeting and exceeding customers needs".

Based on what we have discussed so far, *service is broadly defined as an exchange of value between the provider and customer.*

The customer is therefore someone we exchange value with. The value received by the customer is what we have discussed in **Service Unusual Practice #5**. Of course, the value is conveyed by the experience the customer goes through with us.

On the other hand, the service provider receives value from the customer in terms of profit and reputation. Not always though.

A participant, who attended a leadership programme in Chiangmai, Thailand, challenged this definition of service by asking what value non-profit service organisations like charities receive. I replied that value received is not always tangible like monetary rewards. People, who start non-profit bodies, set out to fulfil higher ideals like eradicating poverty, illiteracy, sickness etc. They derive value from a sense of fulfilment of having achieved (or at least progressed towards) these goals. They are motivated by a higher order need for self-actualisation (according to the well-known Maslow's hierarchy of needs).

Not happy with my reply, he further asked, as a father, what value could he get from having and raising a child? As a parent, he expects nothing back in return from his child. Therefore there is no exchange of value between parent and child.

I threw back at a question at him: "When you were holding your new-born in your arms, how did you feel?"

He was stunned for a moment. He then sheepishly answered: "Proud."

"What else?" I probed.

"I look forward to coming home every night so that I could see him." Sounds like he has gained a renewed sense of purpose in life.

I then hammered in the point: "How different are you now and before you became a father?"

"Well, I am more focused on my work and family life because there are more people dependent on me."

"Do you like yourself better because of this focus?"

"Yes."

Bingo! There is value from being a parent. He has gained a higher sense of self-worth and responsibility.

Call me a doomsayer but we live in a very pragmatic world. If you don't add value, you are out!

Personal Practice Tips:

- Pay attention to and monitor your customer retention rate calculated by the percentage of revenue derived from repeat purchases. Another way to look at retention is to calculate your churn (turnover) rate: percentage of customers who leave you within a time period.

- If your customer retention rate is falling, find out why by talking to current and ex customers.

- Ask how you are doing compared to your competitors. Are they winning over your customers?

- Determine how you can lower your customer costs. Besides keeping an eye on your production and operation costs, more importantly, make sure your customers find it convenient and hassle-free to deal with you before, during and after the purchase.

- Enhance your customer benefits by providing add-on services that your competitors do not.

- Constantly build on your reputation and image (a customer benefit) so that your customers will continue to have confidence in buying from you.

- Do not over-rely on pricing to win and keep customers. Work on lowering other customer costs and increasing customer benefits instead.

SPOTTING THE RIGHT
SERVICE STRATEGY

"In the end, there is no greater failure in strategic thinking
than the failure to choose, to make the tradeoffs necessary
to distinguish you from your competitors."

MICHAEL PORTER, AUTHOR OF *COMPETITIVE STRATEGY*

Strategy, simply put, is a plan of activities to achieve a goal. As Michael Porter aptly explains, the plan is to differentiate us from our competitors.

The key in differentiation lies in the discipline of focus. We cannot be all things to all people. We cannot expect to attract and please all customers. World-class businesses get to where they are by zooming in on their targeted customer groups. Microsoft sticks to software though there were temptations in the past to venture into hardware. Wal-Mart is religiously devoted to its "Everyday Low Price" philosophy. Companies that get too adventurous pay the price.

When organisations talk strategy, it is mostly a corporate initiative looking at the business and organisational direction. Here, we are advocating that beyond corporate and business strategies, we need a compelling service strategy to show us how to serve the customers that are brought in as a result of corporate strategies.

Service Usual Practice #6:
We need to invest in and provide "good" service to compete.

Service **Unusual** Practice #6:
There is no good service, only the right service. Right service is good service.

Service is in the Eye of the Beholder

There is a new restaurant in town. Many of your friends have dined there and passed comments to say the place has excellent food and service. You decide to try the restaurant out only to find that the food is bland and your order is wrongly taken.

What is good value and service to you might be just average to the next person. Customer value and service are extremely subjective. Ask the locals where we can find the best Tom Yam Kung soup in Bangkok and be confused by the flood of answers. The most common answer is probably "At home". Everyone has different preferences. Some like it hot and spicy. Some insist on adding coconut milk to the soup. Therefore the best soup can be found at home where you have free rein to customise the dish to your exact taste.

Choosing Our Customers

We have discovered that service and value is subjective; to each its own. To gain customer delight with our service, we therefore need to ensure that we are targeting the right service to the correct customer groups. Coming back to Michael Porter's assertion that strategy is a matter of focus and choice, it is extremely trying, if not impossible, to spread ourselves thin trying to attract and retain different market segments with a wide range of services.

Southwest Airlines is a pioneer budget airline in the United States. It was started in 1971 and has achieved 31 consecutive years of profitability. Since the beginning, it has stuck to a simple service strategy: if you get your passengers to their destinations on time, at the lowest possible fares, and make darn sure they have a good time doing it, people will fly your airline. Over the years, while its competitors have been tempted to twitch their strategies to provide different service levels (for example, business class) to more customer segments (business travellers), Southwest Airlines has never wavered from its core service purpose. In May 1988, it was the first airline to win the coveted Triple Crown for a month – Best On-time Record, Best Baggage Handling, and Fewest Customer Complaints among all US airlines. Since then, they have won it more than 30 times.

An organisation cannot be all things to all people. To excel, it has to select the types of customers it wants to serve. Both McDonald's and the Mandarin Oriental are reputed for their services. While McDonald's specialises in fast and efficient delivery, The Mandarin Oriental hotel is known for its intimate and warm pampering.

Provide too little service, and of the wrong kind, and customers will leave.

Provide too much, even of the right kind, and the company will either go broke or price itself out the market.

Budget airlines are the rave today. They do not serve drinks or meals (unless you pay for them). Seats are smaller. Legroom is squeezed. There is no assigned seating in most cases. In the conventional sense, budget airliners do not provide much or "good" service. But their prices are way below their regular competitors, as much as 50 per cent or more. They attract short-haul price-conscious travellers who do not mind the lack of service in exchange for lower prices. To these customers, there is still value due to low prices. To these airlines, there is value due to low operating costs.

On the other hand, long-haul and business travellers would prefer to pay much more to enjoy good food, better seats and entertainment.

What we are seeing here is that not only do our customers get to choose us, we get to choose our customers too! If we are clear and focused on who we want to attract, we will learn to turn away customers outside our target scope. In recent years, banks having been moving towards automating their services with ATMs, cash deposit machines, internet banking etc while shutting down costly branches. Part of their intent, besides cost savings, is to switch their customer focus to a younger, more highly-educated population who are at the peak of their income-generating capacity. They belong to the customer segment that is able and willing to use technology. Left on the sidelines are the older customers who are not as technology-savvy. They are crying foul over longer queues at fewer banking locations.

Segmenting Our Services

James L. Heskett of Harvard Business School defines segmentation as "the process of identifying groups of customers with enough characteristics in common to make possible the design and presentation of a product or service each group needs".

Segmentation is already common in our marketing department. Marketers are clear about the need to focus. But our marketing segmentation tends to focus on *customer needs*. This allows us to choose our customers. A Japanese department store like Seibu aims for high-worth customers who demand attention and prestige while Giant and Carrefour are discounters meant for the masses who are price-conscious.

What is more rare is service segmentation, where the focus is on *service expectations or dimensions*. Hence in service segmentation, a different model is required. In a restaurant business, marketers would classify customers into categories like business people, families, youth etc. The restaurant manager, however, will recognise entirely different segments among the customers: those who are in a hurry, those who are particular about the taste etc. Service segmentation is thus a second layering of our selected market segments based on how these segments want to experience the service.

We usually fear two segmentations of the same market, but this concern is unwarranted. Those marketers responsible for acquiring new customers use market segmentation during the purchase stage. A service segmentation is for those who serve customers, and are unable to adapt to every individual need but unwilling to treat all customers the same during the experience delivery stage.

Several service segments may exist within one market segment. One customer service segment can also cut across several market segments.

The two forms of segmentations can be further explained by the following example. We look at MK Restaurants, a leading suki/hot-pot restaurant chain in Thailand with over 170 outlets, known for its efficient service and reasonable pricing.

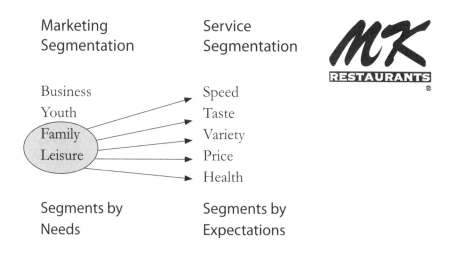

MK restaurants have various possible customer segments: Business, Youth, Family and Leisure. Each customer segment has its own needs. Business executives need to impress their clients and associates in a pampered and undisturbed setting. Families require the restaurant to be kid-friendly. At the strategic and marketing level, MK has decided to focus on primarily meeting the needs of the Leisure and Family segments.

But within the selected Leisure and Family customer groups, the customers have different expectations on how they want to experience the restaurant. Some want the service to be fast (speed). Others judge the restaurant by the quality of food (taste). Still others value more variety of items on the menu. Some want to be sure that the food served is nutritious and healthy. To top it off, most expect affordable pricing.

That is why when you visit an MK restaurant; you are greeted with efficient and fast service with little frills. The menu is standardised.

The food quality is consistent. So is the service behaviour of the well-trained staff. The heating stove is of industrial strength; the hot pot will boil in a matter of minutes. You can expect a quick turnaround of tables even on busy days. You will also find word puzzles for children and fact sheets on food nutrition on each table. The food you have just consumed will be broken down by nutrients and calories in a list that will accompany your bill. Best of all, the bill will not burn a hole in your pocket.

MK is doing a great job trying to satisfy most, if not all expectations of its selected customers. Yet, at its core, what service dimensions make MK stand out from its competitors in the eyes of its customers?

Service Strategy

To answer this question, we can perform a simple assessment. We rate each of the identified service expectations against three criteria known as the 3 Cs:
• Capabilities/Competencies
• Customer Profitability
• Competition

Capabilities/Competencies

We have to consider our current and potential capabilities in serving a particular segment. MK has always been known for its efficiency and fast turnaround of tables. It is able to offer a 5-minute guarantee: from order placed to the arrival of the food. On the other hand, to ask MK to serve businessmen who expect fine dining is a stretch. We allocate points (0-lowest to 100-highest) according to how able our capabilities and competencies are to meet the expectations of the particular service segment. If we do not possess the capabilities at present, we can still give ourselves high points if we possess the potential to develop those competencies.

Customer Profitability

Can we benefit from serving the chosen segment? Sophisticated companies always seek to serve customers who are less costly to serve and have attractive future buying potential. These customers are deemed high value. This criterion looks at our ability to serve the segment profitably. Unlike customer value, we now turn the value question to ourselves. What costs must we expend to earn the benefits from the customers?

Do not expect free alterations if you buy clothes from a discount store. On the other hand, you will get free personalised advice on top of tailor-fit alterations at Giorgio Armani. Of course, the price differential between the two stores is glaring. You can afford to offer free alterations if the customer is willing to "pay" – the cost is already built into the original selling price.

Good value means gaining benefits from the customer under favourable terms, taking into account both the financial and non-financial costs.

The ATM is a good example. It reduces the cost of servicing customers and at the same time, frees up the bank tellers to serve more technology-challenged customers like elderly folks. Manpower and branches can be reduced. For most customers, long queues are a thing of the past and they have access to the bank services 24 hours a day. Looks like a win-win situation for most of us, except for some die-hards who miss the personal touch.

The Asian Banker Research estimates that the average ratio of self-service transactions to total transactions for medium to large-sized Asian retail banks is about 45 per cent. Some banks, however, have already brought self-service transactions to at least 70 per cent of total. These banks are already seeing the benefits of keeping the level of self-service transactions high. Kasikornbank in Thailand has reduced average staff per branch from 23 to eight. The bank has brought self-service transactions to 75 per cent of total transactions.

Points for this criterion are awarded on the basis of the potential returns versus the potential costs of serving a particular segment. More points are given for better relative returns to costs. MK's meals are not pricey. It invests heavily in technology. Its staff now use palm-tops to take and process orders. This has increased its productivity by reducing manpower. The saving is passed onto its customers with lower prices. With its industrial-strength heating stoves and standardised operational processes, MK is able to achieve high turnaround rates to serve more customers.

Competition

No segmentation can be complete without considering how our competitors are positioning themselves against us. Strategy is about differentiation. Service is no different. Understanding where competitors are in the life cycles of their customer service operations leads to more intelligent strategic choices. The analysis should steer us away from copycat strategies that yield little or no returns.

Competitors here refer to those competing in the same market segments. Higher points are given to those service segments in which we have a clear advantage over its competition. MK's food cost less than its long-time rival Coca Suki. Thus MK commands more points under Price with this criterion.

The assessment is shown in the form of a table below:

Selected Customer Segments of MK: FAMILY, LEISURE

Possible Service Segments	Capacities/ Competencies (0 to 100)	Customer Profitability (Cost vs Benefits)	Competition (0 to 100)	Total Score (out of 300)
*Speed	90	70	80	240*
Taste	70	70	60	200
Variety	70	70	60	190
*Price	70	60	90	230*

Key Service Segments: TASTE & PRICE

The 3 criteria are given equal weightings given the assumption that all 3 criteria are similarly crucial in the consideration of service segmentation. However, some industries might require different weightage for the criteria. For example, if competition is not intense, more weightage can be given to the other criteria.

The service expectations or dimensions, with the highest number of points out of a maximum of 300 points, are deemed key or core and constitute the service strategy.

In the MK example, we evaluate 4 service segments: **Speed**, **Taste**, **Variety**, and **Price**. We shall leave Health aside for now as we can assume that all customers are generally conscious of what they eat. The conclusion from this analysis is: Price and Speed are the key service dimensions of MK. MK has the competency and competitive edge to concentrate on these two areas. In addition, these two areas yield better returns in relation to the costs of providing them. They are what make customers come back. Although MK does not neglect the other expectations of taste, variety and health, it zooms in strongly on its service strategy of *good food with responsive service at good prices.*

The bottom-line is that to be world-class, we need to adopt a concise service strategy that *tells us how to provide the intended service experience to our identified customers who are earlier picked out by our corporate and marketing strategies. A good service strategy dictates that our service experience focuses on a few key service dimensions like speed, price etc.* while not neglecting others. We excel in a few areas while remaining competent in the rest.

Here are some examples of service strategies:

Singapore Changi Airport, consistently voted one of the best airports in the world:

> To be the BEST and FRIENDLIEST airport in the world by using the four values in F.A.C.E. and realising each individual counts.
>
> Flexible   Attentive   Courteous   Efficient

> Richard Branson's Virgin:
>
> Brand Values:
> • Genuine and Fun
> • Contemporary and Different
> • Consumers' Champion
> • First Class at Business-Class Prices

L.L. Bean, a leading direct marketer of merchandise in the United States:

"Sell **good** merchandise at a **reasonable** profit, treat your customers like **human beings**, and they'll always come back for more."

Even public bodies have service strategies. After all, they exist to serve the public. This one is by a tax authority of an Asian country. They are aware that the public does not actually want to constantly deal with them (since they 'suck' money from the public). They aim to keep the need for the public to have to deal with them to a minimum. Led by this service value, they implement electronic tax filing, phone tax filing, and automatic income reporting from the employers (eliminating the need for the public to fill in their income figures):

"Our commitment to quality is to achieve customer satisfaction at <u>one</u> and <u>only</u> one encounter."

Service Dimensions

We learnt that the service strategy contains a set of chosen service dimensions which determines how we want to serve our chosen customers. When we segment services, we do so according to the service characteristics expected. We call them service dimensions. As seen earlier in the example of MK, service dimensions are derived from the service segments. If a particular service segment expects a great deal of individual attention, the service dimension would need to reflect this personalisation.

Again, the key is to keep things simple and practical yet differentiating. Good service strategies contain only a few core service dimensions. For example, when customers are asked to describe McDonald's, attributes like Speed and Efficiency come to mind. Mention Thailand and descriptions like Hospitality and Value for Money are commonly used. Again, while we want to be known and defined by our key service dimensions, we have to ensure that other non-core service dimensions are maintained and present throughout our service experience. McDonald's must ensure that its food is hygienic and palatable. Visitors to Thailand can leave with a bad experience if they face constant inefficiencies like traffic jams and long waits.

What are service dimensions? Parasuraman, Zeithaml and Berry, authors of the definitive book on service quality, *Deliver Service Quality*, determine that the service experience can be expressed in 5 core service dimensions known by the acronym **R.A.T.E.R:**

Reliability - The ability to perform as promised, dependably and accurately.

Assurance - The knowledge and courtesy of employees, and their ability to convey confidence and trust.

Tangibles - The physical appearance and image of facilities, equipment peripherals and personnel.

Empathy - The degree of caring and individualised attention provided.

Responsiveness - The willingness to help and provide prompt service.

These are core dimensions. Other commonly used service dimensions used are:

Flexible, Price, Innovative, Value, Fun, Simple, Anticipatory etc.

Personal Practice Tips:

- Don't expect to attract and please every customer.

- Conduct an assessment to determine the market and service segments to focus on by following the steps below:

Step 1: Determine the market segments to target. This segmentation is based on customer needs.

Step 2: Brainstorm all possible service segments based on customer expectations. You can come up with these segments by observing and talking to existing customers.

Step 3: Evaluate each possible service segment using the 3Cs evaluation criteria. Each criterion has a total of 100 points to be allotted to each service segment. Assign weightage to the criteria if necessary.

Step 4: Tally the total score for each service segment (out of 300 points) and use the total scores as a basis to decide the service segments to focus on.

- Create a service strategy statement consisting of the core service dimensions associated with the selected service segments.

Chapter

6

DOING BUSINESS WITH OUR PEOPLE

"If you want to be prosperous for a year, grow grain.
"If you want to be prosperous for ten years, grow trees.
"If you want to be prosperous for a lifetime, grow people."

CHINESE PROVERB

We now have the right strategy. It is time to execute the service experience.

Enter our people. They are the means to execution and implementation. They are responsible for creating and delivering the service experience. We all know this for a fact. Management gurus have been telling us for years that people are our greatest resource, who need to be nurtured and motivated so that they will yield returns for us.

Are we assuming that our people are going to stand still and be developed and motivated by us? No. People are more mobile and self-reliant today. Gone are the days when they will stay in a job for life. They have more options in today's diverse economy. Conversely, there is no longer any life-long job guarantee to be found among employers. Even the Japanese, who used to pride themselves on life-long employment, are finding out that jobs today have limited life spans.

The way we look at selecting, equipping and retaining our employees must change.

Service Usual Practice #7:

Our employees are our greatest assets. We should work towards developing and then retaining them.

Service **Unusual** Practice #7:

We do not own our employees. We should focus on developing and retaining only those who can add value to us and to whom we can add value.

Loyalty Revisited

I was posted to Hong Kong to be the country manager of a regional logistics company. The business unit there had already been operating for a number of years. I took over during a time when the company was computerising its scheduling function. Before that, route scheduling was done manually under a manager. This change required the manager and his team to learn to use the computer.

Change is never easy for any one of us. It was particularly difficult for this manager. He, in his 50s, had been with the company for about 10 years. He was hoping to ride out this job without fuss and retire in a few years.

Unfortunately change found him and spoilt his self-imposed tranquillity. I recommended that he attend the computer training with his team. He refused, claiming that he did not want to be seen learning with his subordinates. I then offered to allow him to be trained separately and individually. He gave me a resigned look and exclaimed that he was too old to learn to use the computer and the new scheduling system.

My patience was starting to wear thin. How would he do his job if he did not learn? I asked. Well, his staff could handle the work, he countered. Short of asking him what he was going to do if his staff were doing all the work, I nonetheless persisted by offering to teach him the computer and system personally for the next few Saturdays when the office was empty. That way, he would have no worry about losing face in front of others.

"Sorry, Saturdays are my family days," He gave me a disdainful look.

Over the next two weeks, I attempted to find alternatives to this problem. I even offered him a transfer to the operations department where he had come from. He rejected the offer, saying he could not get along with the people there. At the end of two weeks, I gave up. I brought the matter to the headquarters and the reply was swift and decisive: ask him to leave with compensation.

My conscience was clear but my guts were a little lacking. I had never fired anyone before. But I had to do what I had to do. I called him into my room. Just when he thought I was going to suggest another crazy idea, I told him that given his stand, the company had no choice but to let him go with full compensation under the local labour laws.

I would never forget his expression at that moment. His jaws literally dropped. He fell backwards into the chair. I had never seen a more shocked look on anyone's face. It was as if the world had come to an end. "But I have done so much for the company for so many years," He gasped.

I stood my ground. When he realised that the decision was final, he stood up, overturned the chair and shouted: "This is how you repay loyalty!" That was the last I saw of him.

I bet my bottom dollar he did not understand the meaning of value. He assumed that the company was going to feed him for the rest of his professional life.

Value of One

How loyal are you (if you are an employee) to your employer? How loyal is your employer is to you?

Trying to answer these two questions will open our eyes to a new paradigm towards our work. We can apply the same understanding of customer value to our work situation. *Loyalty is Dead!* We should see ourselves as our own bosses. This applies to all of us, regardless of whether we are business owners or employed by others. We own a business. This business employs one and only one person: us as individuals. What does our business offer? It sells our services: time, skills, experience, expertise and even commitment (often mistaken for loyalty).

Our employers are our customers. They buy our services in exchange for giving us salaries, fringe benefits, learning and growth opportunities, status etc. They, as customers, have a right to pick whom to buy and not buy from. If at any time, we are deemed to be costing our employers more than we are benefiting them, we are out! Layoffs and retrenchments are commonplace today.

On the other hand, we are no sitting ducks either. If we perceive that we are not getting a fair deal out of the work relationship, we will not hesitate to bide our bosses farewell. We, too, have a right to choose our customers.

We are a "value of one". We are a single, independent, value-adding unit. We seek to give and receive value at all times. We accept that at any time the value received does not commensurate with the value given; our relationship with our customer is in jeopardy.

Therefore the initiative now lies with the employee to manage his/her own career to ensure that he/she is in demand with prospective employers. Employers can only facilitate by providing the right encouragement, environment and incentives. These employers cannot force development down their throats.

Different Strokes

It is all about finding the right people for the right job. If the fit is there, the service experience will be excellent. If the fit is absent, cut our losses and part with each other. I have actually encountered a couple of situations in which the people I fired came up to me a few years after and thanked me for being honest about their non-suitability. Of course at that time when emotions ran high, I was their public enemy number one. But after the dust had settled over time, the same people could objectively see that they would be wasting their time and the organisation's if they had stayed on. Therefore we can, unashamedly, expect our employees to add value to us, their customers. Value can be sales, time and costs saved, taking up the slack to free us to focus on our core work etc. If this value is not forthcoming, we can seek it elsewhere.

On the other hand, having found the right people, we cannot presume the right that we own them, like assets. Our employees have a right to walk out on us at any time. We must accept that. We must reciprocate by adding value to them so that they can continue to add value to us. Value, in this case, is more than monetary incentives. It can be learning opportunities, career development etc. It is also our responsibility to develop our employees' potential to add value. They gain capabilities and competencies. We profit from their increased contributions. Everyone is happy.

While we are clear about how our employees can add value to us, what is of value to employees is subjective. Different employees look to get different benefits out of the employment relationship.

To make sense of the different expectations of employees, we first need to distinguish between the different modes of services and the type of employees who work in each mode. Services can be considered along two dimensions:

Customisation

Certain services need to be tailored according to individual needs. Consulting, medical treatment, technical support and interior design are examples of personalised services. Even then, the degree of customisation varies. Visiting a tailor to make a suit and altering an off-the-rack suit both require customisation. Obviously, the tailor will make a one-of-kind suit to conform to only your body contour. On the other extreme, fast food outlets and clothing outlets offer predetermined menus and sizes. Take it or leave it. There is little or no exception. The more customisation, the more the employees must probe customers, analyse needs, identify problems, provide solutions, answer objections. Such intensive services, either once or repeatedly over time, will require service personnel who can stand on their feet, react quickly, and independently make decisions without consulting their superiors.

Interactions

The frequency and duration of contacts between the customer and service provider vary with services. Some services require a long duration of contact. Dealing with a consultant could go on for hours. Other services need brief, but frequent, contact. A hotel guest could have a total of five minutes of contact with the different hotel staff spread out over a few days. The longer the duration and the greater the frequency of contact, the more the service organisation needs to ensure a consistent level of quality in the various encounters, whether the customer is handled by a single employee repeatedly or by different people at different times. A service can require either an extended contact with a particular person like a counsellor, or a series of short but frequent dealings with different staff members like in a hospital.

Based on the two dimensions of customisation and interactions, we can derive four types of service operations:

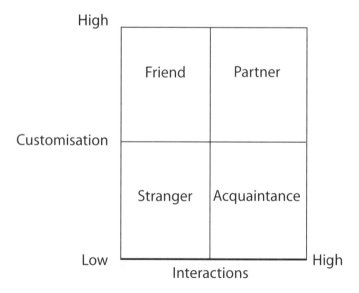

The Four Types of Service Operations

Stranger

Here the service interaction is short and superficial. There is no planned customisation. Staff do not need a profound knowledge of the service or the customer. Skilled staff are the least necessary for services of this type. The people component of the service encounter is less important than the process's efficiency. Services that fall under this type are fast food restaurants, supermarkets, retailers and leisure parks.

Acquaintance

The service involves long and/or frequent but little personalised contacts. Staff will need to know the customer a little but not well. They must have product and company knowledge, be able to answer questions, resolve problems which have been delegated to their level and solve customer complaints. Hotels and restaurants are typical examples.

Friend

The customer is treated like a friend. Interactions are short and infrequent but highly personalised. A person drinking alone at the bar might need some chatting and personal gestures from the bartender. A call reporting the loss of a credit card to the call-centre would require a service provider to know how to listen and respond to the problem immediately. Call centres hotline operators and bars are examples.

Partner

These services are the most involved. Such services demand long and frequent interactions with a high level of customisation. Contact staff must not only be able to stand on their own and react, but also to develop a relationship with the customers over time. Social skills like listening, knowing and anticipating needs, empathy and sympathy become more important as the duration of contact increases. Professional and technical services like consulting are examples of this form of service.

The names of each of the four types of operations reflect the degree of involvement between the customer and the service provider. Each service operation requires a different calibre of employees who need to be developed, managed and motivated differently.

Our service people strategy is all about selecting, equipping and retaining the right people for the right service. That way, we ensure that we find the right employees who can add value to us and whom we can add value to.

Paying a professional a high salary but giving him/her only routine work is not adding value to the person who is probably seeking fulfilment in the work. Nor are we deriving the maximum value from the person. Both sides lose. So is paying a high school kid minimum wage to supervise a fast-food crew. The kid's responsibility is way above what he is capable or willing to accept while all he wants is to earn some money to buy the latest Nike sneakers.

Much like our service strategy, we cannot be all things to all people. We are not equally capable of providing all four types of development, management and motivation to our employees. We have to be clear about what service type we belong to and gear our people policies and practices to attract and keep the appropriate employees.

	Stranger	Acquaintance	Friend	Partner
Employees	Young or retirees. Part-timers. Can take instructions.	Possess some professional technical skills. Reliable and consistent.	Professionals with specialised skills. Responsible and trustworthy.	Professionals with technical and people skills. Independent and enjoy making decisions.

	Stranger	Acquaintance	Friend	Partner
Development	Basic training on procedures.	Orientation, basic skills training and on-the-job training. Work coaching.	Learning new techniques. Job rotation. Job enrichment. Work coaching.	Developing leadership competencies and soft skills. Job enrichment. Mentoring.
Management	Close supervision.	Managers allow input from employees but make the ultimate decisions.	Managers coach employees who are given the authority to make decisions with input from managers.	Managers delegate authority and responsibility to employees without need to be involved.
Key Motivation	Pay. Camaraderie of fellow employees.	Pay. Career advancement.	Recognition. Learning opportunities. Work challenges.	Freedom for self-expression. Recognition. Internal promotion to leadership positions. Work challenges.
Empowerment	No or little empowerment.	Empowerment on common customer issues. Beyond that, there is a need to bring the matter to higher authority.	Broad empowerment. Escalation to higher authority on exceptions only.	Almost boundless empowerment.

But in reality, within the same organisation, there can be different departments and functions that operate like the four service types. The marketing department typifies "Friend" services while the finance department might operate like a "Stranger" or "Friend". In a retail bank, for instance, tellers play the role of a "Stranger" while personal wealth managers act like a "Partner". This necessitates a flexible and differentiated set of people policies within a single organisation to cater to the different expectations. We need to specialise in working with the people who can match our service type and yet be good enough to deal with others of different expectations.

When Bad Service is Good

Having employees with the right fit will enable the service experience to be extraordinary. Tsui Wah Restaurant has nine outlets in Hong Kong. The most prominent one is found in Central, the business district of Hong Kong. Because of its location, it attracts patrons from all walks of life: business tycoons, celebrities, office workers, ladies of leisure and even labourers working at nearby construction sites etc.

Eating at Tsui Wah is certainly an experience. On any given weekday during lunchtime, you see the waiters bustling around, making friendly banter with some regular patrons: "Is that a new watch you are wearing, Mr. Leung?", "Liverpool is going to lose by at least two goals to Manchester United!"

But when you glance over to another area of the restaurant, you are likely to see tables where empty plates lie uncollected. The teacups are not topped up. The waiters seem to avoid these tables while paying attention to others.

Yet, the owner of the restaurant chain is proud of the fact that he has spent significant amounts of money on training his staff in customer service, communications, team building and food & beverage knowledge.

So what is happening? On the surface, you might think that the service is inconsistent with some customers getting better service than others. But actually, the waiters are practising *discretion*. When they see businessmen engrossed in conversations or couples arguing, they learn to leave them alone and not interrupt them. They are aware that nothing annoys businessmen more than when a chirpy waiter goes up to them and asks if everything is all right while they are in the midst of negotiating a multimillion dollar deal. If these customers need service, they will ask for them. There are also occasions when the waiters see regular customers walking in with their arms wrapped around companions who are not their spouses. In these situations, they remain cordial without being too familiar and inquisitive. But when regular customers come in alone, the attention showered on them can be overwhelming.

Such discretion cannot be learnt through training alone. The owner has to firstly recruit the right people who are emotionally sensitive to others. Most of all, the service staff are encouraged to use their discretion to provide the service experience.

Tsui Wah Restaurant in Central, Hong Kong

Personal Practice Tips:

- Determine the type of service operation you belong to according to the degree of customisation and interaction. Base your people policies and practices on the appropriate service type.

- Recruiting the right people is more than half the battle won. Allocate more time and resources to this step.

- Recruitment is never an exact science. A surer way to test if an employee is able to add value is during the probation period. Extend the period if the employee shows potential but needs more time. If you are sure the employee does not fit, part amiably during the period.

- You cannot develop people. You can only help develop them. Emphasise to employees that ultimately, they must own the initiative to take care of their own careers and not rely on the company to groom them. You can facilitate their development by providing learning opportunities through training, job enrichment/rotation, and career advancement. But they must decide if they want to capitalise on these opportunities.

- Be prepared to lose employees who are not getting value from you by way of rewards or development. Remember, you cannot be all things to all people. It is better to separate and remain friends than be miserable together.

- You need to be cruel to be kind. If the employee is not adding value due to lack of either ability or motivation in spite of your best efforts to develop and manage him/her, it is best to be honest with him/her. He/She might even thank you for this one day. If you are so inclined, you can help outplace the person in another job. Do not "emotionalise" the issue unnecessarily.

- Use a Coach approach in managing your people. People today respond better to a more consultative and empowering approach from bosses. Guide and support rather than instruct.

- Link rewards and incentives to behaviours that encourage initiative and customer-focus.

Chapter

7

ENABLING WITH PROCESS/PRODUCT

"Drive thy business or it will drive thee."

BENJAMIN FRANKLIN

Even our best people need direction and the how-to to serve our customers. Our procedures, systems and policies drive the way we do business.

Process refers to the procedures, rules, regulations, policies, systems that an organisation follows in executing its business and operation.

Products, in the form of technology, equipment and tools, are intertwined in our processes today. Many processes and systems are highly dependent on technology to drive them. Thus, we shall discuss process and product in the same breath here.

Be careful every time you use phrases like "Sorry, this is our company policy" or "This is how we do things around here all this while". These are trigger words to the customer's anger and frustration. You know what I mean. Benjamin Franklin was right (amazing since he said this in the 1700s). If we do not watch out, the rules and systems that we create will end up controlling us.

So how do we learn to control and manage this "process monster"?

Service Usual Practice #8:
Our service processes and products should be designed "outside-in" with the customer in mind.

Service Unusual Practice #8:
Our service processes and products should be designed "inside-out" with our people in mind so that they can be enabled to serve our customers better.

Sally's Sad Story

Sally was an account executive with a design house specialising in designing and producing promotional and marketing material for corporations. Her job was to manage and service about 10 of the house's major clients.

She was the crucial link between the clients and her company. She would liaise with her clients, hear their needs, convey these needs to her creative design colleagues, bring back ideas and concepts to the clients, work to get an agreement, have the designers make the necessary changes, co-ordinate with the printers on the production of the materials, ensure that the quality was on-par and the delivery was on-time, and at all times, keep her clients informed and happy.

Time is money as we say. Sally's employer was well aware of this. In this cut-throat industry, clients want their needs met fast and cheaply. To be more customer-focused, Sally's boss decided to shorten the usual service process by consolidating the production function to three preferred printers. To ensure proper co-ordination, a production executive position was created to handle and manage all production matters. Sticking with three preferred printers meant these printers would be able to offer better prices due to economies of scale. The design house would then pass on part of the cost savings to its clients.

Sally used to be able to use any of the dozen or so printers the house worked with. She had the flexibility to decide who to use and when. She knew which printer was better at certain types of work and quantities. Some printers were more adept at last-minute rush jobs than others. With the new policy of using only three printers, Sally lost that flexibility. She could no longer go direct to the printers. She had to work through the production executive. When she brought this concern up to her boss, he assured her that by freeing her up from production matters, she could better concentrate on liaison with her clients.

Sally begged to differ. Her job required her to provide a personalised service to her clients. What her clients wanted from her was direct and fast answers. She could offer all that only if she was in control of all aspects of the work. However, now, whenever a client asked about the status of the production or made a sudden change in specifications, she had to check with the production executive who had to deal with all other clients' productions. Naturally, this person would be slower to respond and worse still, not inclined to be flexible since he was not directly accountable to the clients. When Sally could not get the right answers fast enough, the clients would sometimes take it out on her.

Sally found that her job was made more difficult. She decided to resign. Her boss was taken aback. He thought with the changes, he had enabled the company to meet its clients' needs better. Sally replied:

"You think the new process allows the company to meet *some* of your clients' needs. But it certainly does not help me meet *all* their needs."

Hand-in-Hand

Our people and processes need to synergise and co-exist to provide our customers with their expected service experiences. The obvious trend today is to streamline and make customer-friendly processes, or what service experts call "outside-in" processes with the external customer as the main consideration. What this trend fails to recognise is that these "outside-in" processes can often hinder and frustrate the internal customers: the customer-interfacing employees. As a result, these people cannot and will not live up to their roles and parts. When that happens, customer service is adversely affected.

Many banks today have resorted to fewer physical branches in order to "encourage" their customers to move into electronic and internet banking. This has often resulted in longer queues in the remaining branches since those customers, who still prefer or need to transact in person, have fewer options to go to. Yet the overworked tellers are also required to cross-sell the increasing variety of financial products that banks are carrying today. On top of that, they are expected to be friendly and fast. For this, we need SuperTellers! People who can smile, serve, solve, sell and be swift. Those of us who try to be and do too many things often end up being the master of none. Ask the tellers and most of them will agree.

While we rely on our processes and technology to ensure that our services are more reliable and responsive, our people's attitudes and actions need to be correspondingly reliable and responsive in order not to hinder the processes from serving their purposes. Processes and technology need people to start, operate, monitor and shut down.

On the other hand, people need processes, systems, technology and procedures to guide and aid them. Like it or not, they are stuck with one another for good!

R.A.T.E.R Revisited

Let us revisit the service dimensions from Chapter 5 on Service Strategy. Parasuraman, Zeithaml and Berry exert that the service experience can be expressed in five core service dimensions known as R.A.T.E.R. How can having the right processes, procedures and systems help with each of the five dimensions?

Reliability - *The ability to perform as promised, dependably and accurately.*

Computers and software allow us to crunch data and numbers more accurately and faster. But if the accountant, who produces the reports, forgets to submit them, there is no reliability whatsoever.

Assurance - *The knowledge and courtesy of employees, and their ability to convey confidence and trust.*

Insurance agents now carry computer notebooks that can calculate and customise insurance solutions on the spot. Wireless communications allow product information to be updated and disseminated more frequently.

But knowledge is more than just information. Experience forms an integral and yet intangible part of knowledge as well. This resides in the person doing the work. In sales, articulating product information and benefits is easy. Sensing and understanding the customer's unspoken needs and concerns require experience that cannot be "systematised" and stored in a database. So is courtesy. An automated voice calling out "Good Morning!" is never as appreciated as a real person warmly greeting you with a smile and eye contact.

Tangibles - *The physical appearance and image of facilities, equipment peripherals and personnel.*

Banking halls today have electronic queuing systems that keep waiting customers informed of the expected waiting time and their status in the queue. However, people are part of this dimension as well. The physical facilities and technology may be impressive. But all it takes is a service provider who is dressed or behaves inappropriately to spoil the good impression.

Empathy - *The degree of caring and individualised attention provided.*

This dimension relies heavily on people and not process/technology. In fact, processes and technology risk negating this dimension. Dissatisfaction from callers to call centres using automated interactive voice systems continue to pile up today. People expect to speak to a human being when they call. Instead they are subjected to a menu of options and pre-recorded information.

I remember rushing to a pharmacy during closing time to pick up some toiletries. I sprinted to the checkout counter only to be told by the stone-faced cashier that I could not buy them because the cash registers were closed for the night. I suggested that I pay in cash and all she needed to do was to enter this transaction the first thing the store opened the next day. But in spite of my passionate pleadings that, I was sure, could move a mountain, she refused to budge. The store policy of using the cash register for all purchases was sacred and had to be obeyed at all costs. To her, I was not a customer but an irritant that was preventing her from going home. The process was fixed and standardised. All that was required to save this customer was for the person in front of me to be flexible and empathetic. Alas, it was not to be.

Responsiveness - *The willingness to help and provide prompt service.*

There are two issues here. Processes and technology can enable services to be prompt and fast. Singapore Changi Airport used to screen passengers' bags before check-in. Passengers had to stop at a security station manned by airport security personnel and lift their bags onto a conveyor belt to be screened by a bulky X-ray machine or hand-held scanner. This security procedure increased waiting time. A check-in passenger had to queue up twice: first at the security station and then at the check-in counters. Recently, the airport installed a baggage screening system which cost S$80 million (about US$47 million). This system screen bags after they are checked in behind closed doors. Waiting time and queues are reduced drastically. On top of that, human error and oversight are eliminated.

However, responsiveness also refers to a willingness to help. This is a mindset issue that is attributed to the human factor. If I know how to help you but I don't want to help you, like the cashier in the pharmacy, there is no positive outcome.

Each dimension requires the perfect co-ordination between man and machine (and processes) to come alive. Thus while we cannot ignore the external customers, our processes must be carefully planned with the internal customers in mind. These processes must actually serve a higher purpose of freeing up our people to take better care of our customers. *Service Unusual organisations will focus on processes and products that are both internal and external customer-friendly because they know that ultimately, these will lead to happier customers all round.*

Fail-Safing

The next logical question to ask is: How do we design processes/ products that will work together to empower our people to bring about the desired service experience?

One answer is to design measures and steps in processes and products that will help to prevent service failures or breakdowns. This is known as Fail-Safing. This means to *"make safe failures or to minimise the chances of failures".* This practice is not new. The Japanese even have a term for it: Poke-Yoke.

Often, we are so absorbed in coming up with faster and more fanciful services that we forget the basic: ensuring consistent service delivery and execution with proactive and preventive contingency actions. A hotel coffee shop in Mumbai, India, decided to offer a 10-minute guarantee for set lunches or else the meal was free. As a gimmick, they decided to place an hourglass, calibrated for 10 minutes, on each table. Once the order was placed, the waiter would activate the hourglass. The idea worked. But it soon became apparent that the kitchen was not able to cope with the demand of time-conscious but hungry patrons. The end result was there were many happy and grinning gastronomically-satisfied patrons who got free lunches. The coffee shop failed to plan for the expected increased patronage. It could have limited the guarantee to a certain number of menu items. Restaurants often take this precaution during lunchtime. They confine the lunch menu to a few set meal options to ensure faster service and turnaround of tables.

Fail-safing is not complicated. A tiny bell attached to the door of a small retail store is one such example. It rings when someone opens the door. It alerts the storekeeper, who might be taking stock at the back, of the presence of someone who might be a potential customer or thief. A checklist is a popular and simple fail-safe tool. It ensures that all required steps, actions and criteria are considered without leaving out any.

By preventing service breakdowns, we shield our people from having to waste unnecessary time and efforts to handle complaints and service recovery. Best of all, our customers will be delighted with as few failures as possible.

Service failures can be traced to two main sources: External Customer and Service Provider. When service goes wrong, it is caused by either the service provider or the customer himself/herself. To be specific, each source can cause breakdowns in three different ways:

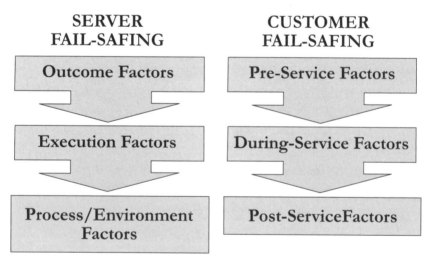

Sources of Service Failures

Fail-Safing the Server (Service Provider)

Outcome Factors

These refer to mistakes made by the service provider that lead to undesired results. What was actually done is not the same as what should have been done. When you send your dented car for body repairs and it comes back with the dent still intact, you are not getting the outcome that you want and expect from the workshop. Failures of this nature can mean outcomes that are incorrect, not as requested, in the wrong order or too slow.

Examples:
Hotels would attach a notice to cleaned laundry that has irremovable stains, stating that they had tried their very best but they could not remove the stains. This is to pre-empt the guests before they spot the stains. The car workshop would call up the owner of the car when they discover a major fault that requires an expensive repair or replacement. They want to keep the owner informed so that there is no surprise when the bill is presented later.

Execution Factors

These are breakdowns that occur during the delivery and execution of the service. The outcomes might turn out as expected but the execution might not. Often these failures are due to the people element. The service provider might neglect to acknowledge, listen or respond to the customer in an appropriate manner.

Examples:
A friend shared with me an experience he had with an international hotel chain. He once arrived at one of their hotels, walked over to the check-in counter, and was greeted immediately by the receptionist with a "Welcome back!" He was curious. "How do you know I have stayed here before without even asking for my identification?" The

receptionist grinned but refused to divulge the secret. Later on, he found out from the general manager that all doormen at the hotel would ask every arriving guest "Is this your first visit with us?" If no, they would signal the check-in counter. A smart, simple yet ingenious way to personalise service.

Process/Environment Factors

These relate to the operational and physical aspects of the service that can go wrong. Let's say you line up to buy a lottery ticket. You get your ticket eventually but you had to wait for over half an hour because there was only one counter open, though there were many buyers in the queue. Dirty toilets, poor lightings, noise, extreme temperatures, odours, sloppy uniforms, error-ridden documents are also tangible impressions of bad service.

Examples:
Hiring extra part-time help during peak periods ensures that the service level is maintained. When was the last time you used the built-in spell check function in the word processing software for important documents? Many hotels conduct line-ups before each shift begins. All staff on that shift would line up for grooming inspection before being released to face the customers. Locker rooms are not short of mirrors to allow the staff to check their attire and appearance before work.

Fail-safing the Customer

Service involves the interaction between customers and service providers. It is a two-way transaction. If one party makes a mistake, the entire transaction can be jeopardised. Customers do make their fair share of mistakes in this relationship.

Pre-Service Factors

These refer to mistakes made by the customers before the exact service transaction. The customers do not prepare themselves properly for the service experience to come. Patients forget to show up for doctors' appointments. The bank loan cannot be processed because an important document was not submitted.

Examples:
Appointment reminders are sent to customers via mail or mobile phone messaging just prior to the appointed day. A checklist of required documents is given to the customer beforehand to help minimise the chance of missing documents.

Tour agencies often conduct briefings for tourists before they depart so that they will know what to expect in terms of weather, schedules, food, activities at the destination. Good restaurants require their waiters to repeat the customers' orders back to make sure there is no mistake in the orders.

During-Service Factors

Customers can cause service breakdowns during the encounter due to inattention, misunderstanding, miscommunication and failure to follow instructions.

I travel a lot. Once during a flight, I needed to go to the lavatory. I saw one that had a green "Vacant" sign so I pushed open the door. Lo and behold! In there was an old lady doing what comes naturally to every person. I quickly looked away, shut the door and apologised profusely though it was not my fault.

Examples:
The universal sign colours on airplanes' lavatory doors are a form

of Poke Yoke. When the sign is red and says "Occupied", we know to wait. Similarly, sufficient, visible and detailed signages in buildings ensure that people can find their way around.

In logistics, "Vendor Managed Inventory" is a concept that has taken root. The main manufacturer of a product would buy parts and components from subcontract vendors to assemble the final product. Whenever the manufacturer requires these parts, the vendor would ship them over. As the vendor might be located halfway around the world, the delivery lead-time could be lengthy. Sometimes the manufacturer would miscalculate the demand and realise, at the last moment, that more parts are needed than initially ordered. However, due to distance and time, the arrival of the parts may be too late to cover the extra demand. The vendors are now fail-safing this by locating their own part manufacturing plants near the manufacturer all over the world. Some practically locate themselves next door to their customers. The vendor would stock and manage all finished parts on behalf of the manufacturer so that the manufacturer does not technically need to hold inventories of such parts. Last-minute urgent demands can be met.

Post-Service Factors

Possible errors made by customers at this stage are the results of the failure to spot service errors, learn from these mistakes, adjust expectations accordingly and execute post-encounter actions. Most customers who encounter service problems would not bother to feedback to the service provider. Thus, the provider remains ignorant and the problems persist.

Examples:
I service my car at a workshop in the neighbourhood. Each time I get my car back, the manager will call me the next day to find out if the car was okay. He will ask me if I was satisfied with the service I received.

This way, he ensures that he has a satisfied customer on his hand. If not, he will at least learn what went wrong. Tax agencies in many countries now allow tax payments to be automatically deducted from the taxpayer's bank account in instalments to facilitate collection.

It is obvious from all the examples above that fail-safing is a lot about common sense. It requires proactive discipline on the part of the organisation to build these measures in their processes to minimise mistakes. Mistakes frustrate both the service provider and the customer. These mistakes lead to an unnecessary waste of time and require resources to rectify. These fail-safe measures thus help to facilitate both the service provider and the customer to successfully execute the service encounter.

Unfortunately, because they can be tedious and mundane, many of us neglect them. We prefer to focus on service expansion, innovation and extension. Usually these involve the use of the latest attention-grabbing technology and gadgets. These generate excitement and attention with the bosses and the customers. They are about doing the right things. Nothing wrong with that. But when we ignore the other side of the equation of doing things right, which is the objective of fail-safing, the end result will not be achieved.

Quick Beauty

A good model of a service organisation that integrates people, process and product seamlessly is QB House of Japan. QB stands for Quick Beauty.

QB was started in 1994 by a 61-year-old businessman, Mr Kuniyoshi Konishi, who came up with the concept for this "just cut" hair salon chain. He observed traditional hair salons and it dawned on him that the reality of a haircut itself does not take much time or cost.

Most of the time wasted results from the stylist moving around the place in search of their tools; serving coffee and tea; and these actions automatically create a long queue for other potential customers.

"The haircut itself doesn't take much time. I felt I was being charged for the time spent on other things as well," says Konishi.

The service value propositions that define QB are therefore speed and price. For just 1,000 Japanese Yen, you can get your hair cut in 10 minutes.

The first **"no-nonsense"** hair salon opened in Tokyo's Kanda district in 1996. Through a franchise system, this hair salon chain grew steadily from 37 shops in 1999 to 57 shops in June 2000, and it has since increased to more than 70 locations spanning across 14 prefectures.

QB House's smooth operations follow what Konishi calls "a crystal-clear system" for shop management. The company is able to integrate the use of process and technology to ensure the highest quality service standards of each store. We will now look more closely at QB's processes.

Internal Processes

- A sensor is fixed on each store's door that allows the head office to know the exact opening and closing times of the store. This sensor thus facilitates the management of store data by the head office.

- Sensors are also used on each salon chair. Each sensor will keep track of the number of customers who occupy the seat each day. Apparently, the sensor will add the customer to its customer tally when he/she has sat down in the chair for at least 6 minutes.

- QB uses ticketing machines to accept payment. Only exact change is allowed. This practice cuts off any human handling of cash and prevents any potential payment and day-end intake discrepancies.

- The ticket vending machines and the chairs are all wired to a main computer for ease of sales monitoring.

- Staff report to work by scanning their fingerprints to monitor attendance. This allows for proper staff control and punctuality while reducing the need for human supervision.

Customer Processes

- To cut down servicing time, QB does not offer the usual shampoo and dry service. Instead it adopts the revolutionary Air Wash method that uses air suction to remove all cut hair fast and effectively without the need to get the customer's hair wet.

- Customers are kept informed of waiting times by colour-coded signals:

  (Red) No waiting necessary.
  (Amber) 5 to 10 minutes of waiting.
  (Green) 15 minutes or more of waiting. (Green)

- QB further differentiates itself with its "one-use" policy that ensures every customer is provided with a new set of towel and comb. In doing so, it gives the perception of hygiene and quality.

- Each chair is sanitised after each use in full sight of the waiting customers.

In 2003, QB expanded to Singapore and Malaysia. There, it introduced a new "shell" concept, that is a portable stand in a cylindrical shape 7 feet high and occupying a surface area of only 40 square feet (3.6 square meters). It contains all the equipment and tools the stylist needs to serve the customer. Its compact design is most suited for congested areas, including airports, train stations, hotels, and shopping centres. The basic service strategy remains the same: "S$10, 10 minutes, Just Cut".

It is obvious that QB relies heavily on processes and technology in its business. Yet through it all, it is ultimately dependent on its human stylists. It is the stylist's skills, behaviour and attitude that determine if the customer is satisfied or not. All the above systems and processes culminate to free up the stylists by removing mundane secondary responsibilities like cash collection and queue management from them. This allows them to complete their work faster and concentrate on serving the customers The processes are "inside-out". They take care of the internal employees so that these employees can take care of customer delight.

Personal Practice Tips:

- Dedicate resources and effort to plan and design the customer interaction flows of your services. Every customer contact point is an experience with you and must be carefully managed. Be as detailed as possible.

- Do not just focus on the service delivery itself. Customers come into contact with us before and after the service delivery as well. Pre and post contact points must be included in the service flow.

- Be aware that the customer can experience us in 3 ways:

1. Physical contact
   This form of contact encompasses all encounters the customer has with respect to our physical and tangible settings: buildings, documentation, signage, merchandise, staff's appearance. This contact directly influences the 5 senses of sight, sound, smell, taste and feel.

2. Transactional contact
   This involves all the interfaces the customer has with our systems and procedures. Here, the customer is concerned with the efficiency of the service.

3. People contact
   This aspect involves dealing with human beings. This is where customers' emotions are invoked by how our people treat them.

All 3 aspects must be looked into when setting the processes.

- Balance your procedures and policies between internal and external customers. Do not please one group by frustrating the other.

- Ensure that the designed processes facilitate and assist the people in the service delivery and not the other way round.

- Minimise service errors by building fail-safe measures in your processes. This requires proactive discipline on your part to always keep an eye on the basics.

- Fail-safing involves the following steps:

  1. Review each stage of the service process and identify where and when potential failures may occur.

  2. Go through 'what-ifs' scenarios and possibilities.

  3. Retrace the process to locate the source of the failure.

  4. Set up a fail-safe system to prevent the mistake.

  5. Monitor the effectiveness of the fail-safe measures.

- Product and Technology used in services are enablers. They exist to support and enhance the services. Do not be tempted to introduce them for their own sake and to impress.

Chapter

8

TAKING THE PROPER MEASUREMENTS

"Barbarism is the absence of standards to which appeal can be made."

JOSÉ ORTEGA Y GASSET (1883–1955),
SPANISH ESSAYIST, PHILOSOPHER

As the popular management maxim goes: "We cannot manage what we cannot measure." Measurement answers the questions: "How are we doing?" and "How did we do?"

Standards of Measurement are indicators that gauge the progress or lack of in any endeavour. Percentage of revenue increase, cost per employee, percentage of customers who are satisfied, response time, number of calls made etc…These are goals that organisations strive towards. They are absolutely necessary. Lacking good measures, no organisation can assess its progress or adjust to changes in customer expectations. No manager can reward employees appropriately and fairly, tune the strategy to customer needs or design product and service processes that bring about service excellence. Without valid measurement systems, it is impossible to know what actions are required to improve customer service.

That is why measurement pervades all the other components of the Service Excellence Pyramid. This component covers the entire perimeter of the pyramid to highlight its prominence (see page 16). All components need to have measures to make them come alive.

Given its importance, how can we ensure the right measurements are effectively in place?

Service Usual Practice #9:

We are intent on putting in place a comprehensive measurement system to track our performance.

Service Unusual Practice #9:

We believe only in measures that can allow our people to buy in and make improvement to our performance.

How To Become Unpopular Overnight

A few years ago, I was appointed the director of a reputable training and consulting company. It had been profitable till shortly before my appointment. I was tasked to help turn it around. Turning around a company requires various considerations: cost reduction, revenue generation, new product development, brand revamp etc. One particularly glaring problem we faced was an ineffective and ill-disciplined sales team of about 12 persons. They were softened by the bountiful years of the past. They came and went as they pleased. There was no sales target or quota. There were no tracking of sales activities.

Being tasked as the leader, I took it upon myself to change things. I introduced a scorecard for each sales person. First of all, I set a sales target for each person. Following that, a series of measures were formalised to account for the sales process: numbers of prospecting, appointments, proposals submitted and sales closures.

Overnight, the sales team realised that the country-club atmosphere and conditions were being replaced by a result-oriented and accountability mode of operations. They were being monitored and scrutinised for every step of their work. Within three months of the scorecard implementation, about one-third of the sales team resigned or asked to be transferred.

Mind you, renewal of people is good at times. It allows for new and fresh perspectives and energy to be injected. But those who left were the better performers. Those who remained continued to play hide-and-seek with me. They tried to avoid me or else bombard me with all sorts of excuses when they could not fulfil their targets and standards: from the poor economy to outdated products/offerings, from lack of support to lack of time. I collected enough excuses to write "1001 ways to get away with not meeting targets" if I wanted to. Most of them were also trainer consultants who spent part of their time delivering workshops. They would start to fill their schedules with more delivery work to avoid selling.

You can imagine that morale was low. The sales team gossiped behind my back. Soon the grapevine blossomed and the whole company knew of me as a cold heartless "Exterminator".

But then again, I remembered someone who once advised me that if I want to be popular, I should be an entertainer, not a leader. So I persisted. Much as I tried, the team was never convinced of the scorecard. However, revenues did go up due to the accountability of the measures. On the other hand, morale never improved and I remained the Hitler of the team. After a year, I was transferred to head another portfolio. Everyone, including I, was happy.

Following me, a veteran director took over. She understood the culture. She immediately abolished the scorecard measures. She even did away with sales targets. The country club spirit came back. The team was smiling more again. She could win any election in the company if ever allowed. Alas, just as you thought this story has a happy ending, it is not to be. Sales went back down. The board got more edgy. That director resigned only after 3 months on the job.

People as Spoilers

Do you think I succeeded? Some of you might think so. Based on the numbers and measures, I had helped bring up the sales figures. I had also made sure that work rates and discipline improved. Others would instead consider me a miserable flop. I had lost some good team players and alienated the rest. Morale and motivation were in the pits. However, my successor experienced contrasting consequences. Happy people but unhappy bosses and poor outcomes.

If you take the perspective from a pure performance measurement angle, indeed I had made good; the numbers had shown positive movements. But if you were measuring employee satisfaction, I would have failed.

That is why Balanced Scorecard, a performance management concept and system devised by Robert S. Kaplan and David P. Norton in 1992, is extremely popular with organisations, both public and private. In Asia, there is a rush towards creating and implementing the scorecard. Among its many benefits is its "balanced" approach: ability to measure not just the financial outcomes, but also the customer, operation and people processes. The Balanced Scorecard would have captured both financial and employee satisfaction outcomes in my case.

Yet, to my knowledge, many scorecard initiatives have either failed or succeeded only partially. Reasons are numerous. Most are directly or indirectly related to people. One key reason is the failure to get people in the organisations to buy in. We do not like to be measured and monitored if we can help it. Measures tie us down and confine us.

Another reason is the complexity and tediousness of the scorecard process. For the scorecard to succeed, it has to be cascaded downwards to all levels of the organisation and eventually end with the individual. All this while, the scorecards from all levels must be linked and integrated with each other. More scorecards mean more measures. We prefer simple, less and easy-to-understand concepts and systems. We lose interest or heart when things get too complicated or numerous. That is why many organisations need to rely on specialised Balanced Scorecard software to manage the scorecards.

People are the key consideration when we plan a measurement system. After all, they are ones executing whatever we are measuring. Unfortunately, many organisations tend to jump onto the bandwagon because such measurement systems infer good management and make for good reporting and accounting to stakeholders like bosses, customers and the public.

Let me end with a take on my story. My scorecard initiative failed because I had not been able to convince the sales team of the intent and need behind the measures. Even the best award-winning scorecard can be undermined if it cannot win over the people who are using it. However, the same scorecard had worked with another team in a previous organisation providing logistics services. In the former case, the sales team in question were well-educated consultants who did not appreciate close scrutiny.

Meeting the Bottom-Line – Rewards, Control and Feasibility

Of course, an obvious way to bring about buy-in is to link rewards and incentives directly to the attainment of the measures. Much as people do not like to be tracked, they know measures are inevitable. Negativity can be neutralised with a carrot when targets are met. Having special awards and incentives for exceeding targets and tying bonuses to key measures are necessary to get the people to take the measures seriously. But rewards and incentives are not a cure-all.

People are equally, if not more concerned about being monitored by the right types of measures within their direct control. Nothing de-motivates us more than being held accountable for a responsibility beyond our control. A waiter, being measured for how long each customer needs to wait after placing the order, would cry foul. The wait depends on how fast the kitchen crew can work. During the SARS outbreak in 2003, many organisations lowered their targets and expectations, recognising that this epidemic was not their doing and out of their influence.

Yet, all is in vain if the data needed to track the measures are unavailable or not feasible to collect. Measures should be selected, in part, based on whether information for the measures is present. If not, a balancing act is called into play: is the measure so important that resources must be expended to facilitate the collection of data? If the answer is no, then scrap the measure. A shoe store attempted to measure how many customers try on shoes as an indication of buying interest. However, every employee would rather concentrate on serving customers than to perform the extra task of keeping tab of shoes tried. Eventually, management decided to invest in hand-held bar code scanners. All shoeboxes were bar-coded anyway for inventory purpose. Now every pair of shoes tried would be scanned. This required minimal effort and did not distract the employees from serving customers.

All measures need to meet the 3 basic criteria of motivation, control and data availability/feasibility to be effective. Once we establish and accept these criteria, we can move on and look closer at how to pick the right measures.

Measuring the Right Dosage

There are 3 different types of measures:

1) Process Measures - these monitor the internal and service processes. They include service standards that are statements of expected performance by employees that are of value to customers. Greeting, Waiting time, Calls per hour etc. In addition, they include people measures like number of training days, employee satisfaction scores etc. They can be operational standards that are quantifiable: waiting time. Or behavioural standards that are observable: "Pass over documents with both hands." They are classified as lead indicators because they are measured before other types of measures. They tend to be found under the Internal Process Perspective (for service standards) and the Learning & Growth Perspective (for people measures) in the Balanced Scorecard.

2) Outcome Measures - these focus on the outcomes of the service processes that an organisation can assess without directly involving its customers. Ideally these measures summarise the effects of the process from the customer's point of view and are closely linked to customer measures. Mystery Shopper's scores, Complaints/Compliments rates, Orders fulfilled within time limit etc. They are still mostly internal measures that can either be classified as lead or lag indicators depending on the level these measures are being evaluated.

At the operating unit, these measures are considered lag indicators that measure end results whereas at the higher corporate level, these measures are still lead indicators to customer measures mentioned next.

3) Customer Measures - these indicate the reactions of existing and potential customers. Ultimately the customer is the judge of what service excellence is. Customer Satisfaction rates, Spending per customer etc. These are lag indicators under the Customer Perspective of the Balanced Scorecard: Market Share, Customer Retention, Customer Acquisition, Customer Satisfaction, and Customer Profitability.

Customer measures concerns stakeholders outside the organisation

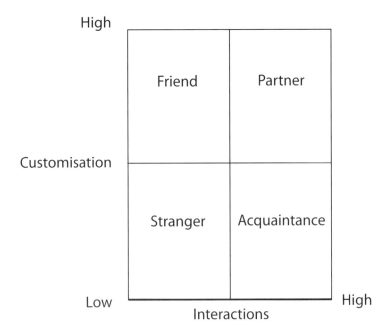

The Four Types of Service Operations

and are touched on in *Chapter 3 on Sensing Our Customers.* Here we shall look into process and outcome measures.

To increase the chance of our people to buy into the measures, we need to use process and outcome measures in different proportions according to the people to be managed. In Chapter 6, we differentiated service into four types, each requiring a different set of service people. We can use this same differentiation to determine how to set the right quantity and combination of process and outcome goals.

Each type of service operations will have its own combination of process and outcome measures as reflected in the following scale:

Stranger
In work that is routine and repetitive, it is best to put in place more process measures such as response time and statements of greeting. The people are more concerned with day-to-day operational issues than final big-picture outcomes like revenue increase. Here, the best combination is maximal, but necessary, process measures and minimal outcome measures. In fact, the people will be lost in the absence of operational and behavioural standards to guide and direct them.

Acquaintance
Here the staffs are more skilled and have longer or more frequent interactions with customers. The level of personalisation and flexibility

in servicing the customers exists but remains low. Thus process measures, though less than that of Stranger, continue to dominate since the focus is still on operations and behaviours. But the staff would need and like to know where all their efforts will lead. Thus a few key outcome and customer measures should be made apparent to help them understand the purpose of their work.

Friend

Work is less routine. Staff are required to use more of their own initiative and capabilities to deal with the customers. Outcome goals such as number of units served or sold per day and percentage of rejects will allow the staff to keep better tab of how they are doing. Process measures, like average time spent with each customer and what to say, become restricting. Staff want and need flexibility in going about their work. If a customer has a complex problem, the person wants the freedom to spend longer contact time with the customer to ensure the resolution is complete without having to watch the clock. Here, outcome measures should dominate. But a few key process measures like making eye contact with the customer at all times or returning all phone calls within the day, should still be in place to ensure consistency in the service experience.

Partner

In this environment, work is highly customised. Routine is thrown out of the window. Staff are required to think on their feet and come up with solutions. There are no or few standard operating procedures to fall back on. To do such work, the people are highly experienced and qualified. They tend to be independent and opinionated. They hate to be bogged down with rules and policies, a.k.a., process measures. They want you to just tell them what their outcome targets are and leave them alone to achieve them.

It is apparent that as the people become more sophisticated and the work becomes more customised or less routine, more outcome measures and less process measures are needed. As mentioned before, an organisation can have different types of operations. Each operation type would need its own concoction of measures.

Applying this understanding back to my earlier account, the training and consulting business is a highly customised one. The sales team was selling solutions, not products. It was a Friend/Partner service operation. Accordingly, the team would respond best to outcome measures. By introducing a scorecard full of process measures, I turned them off. The same scorecard worked with the sales team selling logistics services because they were more in the Acquaintance mode offering rather standardised courier and transportation packages.

Silo Mentality

Another measure implementation problem faced by service usual organisations is the tendency of people to perform to whatever measures are picked, at the expense of the larger reasons for measuring things. Many people incline towards a silo mentality where they are only concerned with their own work and miss the big picture. A service counter staff is measured by whether she smiles or not. Yet, she can be so poor in product knowledge that she will often smilingly tell customers: "I don't know." No amount of smiling will help. This is usually prevalent when there are many process measures that are too narrow in scope. To minimise this silo mentality then, a series of counter-balance outcome and customer measures must be set to focus the service staff on the big picture: the customer.

In the same light, we need to constantly ask ourselves: Are the measures aligned and consistent with each other? If not, these conflicting measures will dilute the overall service effort. For example, a call centre used to measure PCA or Percentage of Calls Answered within 20 seconds. Its target was 95 per cent, which it achieved most of the time. However, the customer survey revealed that customers were not happy with the service. Upon further probing, management found out that because the service staff were so preoccupied with achieving the PCA target, they were hurrying their calls in order to free themselves up to answer as many calls as possible within the target time. Customers' issues were often left unresolved. Management subsequently eliminated the PCA measure and replaced it with Percentage of 1st time Resolution measure.

Thus, measures must be carefully thought through before being introduced. Inputs should be gathered from the employees who are being measured. Importantly, they must be customer-oriented. Remember my encounter with the cashier at the pharmacy? The policy of all transactions going through the cash register was sound but not customer-friendly.

The silo mentality will render any measurement system toothless. It will look good on paper. The numbers on these reports can show if we have progressed or digressed. But in practice, inconsistent and silo measures will frustrate people and worst of all, impede service performance. K-Mart, a major discount retailer in the U.S., used to ask all their checkout clerks to say "Thank you for shopping K-Mart!" The clerks instead responded by blurting "T.Y.F.S.K." (acronym of the statement). Technically, they were following the standard. On the performance management scorecard, this target would be met. In actuality, the customers thought the clerks were speaking a foreign language.

Service Unusual organisations are clear that measurement is ultimately intended to help them improve. They pick the right quantity and types of measures that will aid their people to perform.

Service from the Heart, not by the Book

I came across a newspaper report in The Sunday Times of Singapore from April 2002 that touched on service standards. Let me share some of the findings:

Many organisations rely on process measures in the form of service standards and operating manuals to help train workers and provide the necessary level of service. Such measures dictate how employees should greet, smile and talk to customers. Any deviation from these standards is a no-no. While consistency in service behaviour and performance is welcomed, customers are getting peeved with all-too-mechanical interactions and inflexible policies.

But things are changing. Even McDonald's, a traditional stickler in operating standards, has been making changes since 2000 in its manual to take into account opinions from the ground and shifting its focus from directing to explaining. More organisations now see non-measure-driven service as the approach to take.

This does not mean that process measures are on the way out. The proportions of process/outcome measures for each of the four types of service operations that we have just discussed still apply. A Stranger service still requires more process measures than a Partner business. Here, we are talking about having fewer measures across the board.

Since service is coming more from the heart and less by the book, it is safe, at this juncture, to poke a little harmless fun at some behavioural service standards that used to rule but are now resting in peace in some measure museum:

"Do you smoke?"

Even if customers are kids, staff at a family restaurant were required to ask the question before checking availability of non-smoking seats.

"Apologise profusely when the customer has waited for 10 minutes or more."

A departmental store demanded this of its entire staff regardless of the cause of the wait.

"When carrying a child, do not lift him up from a standing position. Crouch till you are on eye level with him before lifting him up."

From a Tokyo Disneyland manual in the 80s.

"Large note received!"

Many cashiers have to shout to their managers whenever a 10,000-yen note is used by a customer in a Japanese store.

"Change the ashtray when 5 cigarette butts have accumulated – not 4, not 6, but 5."

A standard for waiters in a pub.

Personal Practice Tips:

- Seek the input of employees, who will be measured, when creating the measurement system. This will help to avoid the silo mentality.

- Achievement of measures must be within the direct control or influence of the people working on them.

- Direct attention to the measures by linking rewards and incentives to them.

- Select only those measures that have the necessary and feasible data to track.

- Determine the right combination of process, outcome and customer measures based on the type of operations.

- Put new measures through a trial. Test them out over a defined period of time to ensure consistency and alignment with other measures. Assure the people that if the new measures are found wanting during the trial, those measures will be eliminated. This will further enhance buy-in.

- Results of the measures are not just for management reporting. They should be shared with the people and analysed for improvements.

- The rule of thumb is to minimise the number of measures. Have the necessary measures in place and no more.

Chapter

9

SERVING UP LEADERSHIP

"The great leader is seen as servant first...."

ROBERT K. GREENLEAF,
AUTHOR OF SERVANT LEADERSHIP

We are now in the final chapter, having left the best for last. Leadership is found at the bottom of the Service Experience Pyramid not because it is the least significant. On the contrary, it forms the foundation and anchor of the entire organisation and its service experience.

Leaders influence all the other components of the service experience already discussed. They shape how we understand and interact with our customers. They choose the customers we want to serve. With that, leaders determine the service strategy and values used to serve the chosen customers. They ensure that the relevant people, processes and products are in place and ready to deliver the service experience. To navigate the organisation, they set up and implement an effective measurement system to keep track of our progress.

More of us are acutely aware of the importance of leadership skills in our work. The number of books, assessments and training programmes on leadership today attest to that. Consistent with the premise of this book, we are going to assert that successful leadership should take a non-conventional perspective.

Service Usual Practice #10:
A leader influences and guides his/her followers in a direction, course, action and opinion.

Service **Unusual** Practice #10:
A leader is a servant to his/her followers.

"Are You the Boss?"

I was running a series of on-site management workshops for a government organisation recently. Every day, the first person I saw was Benson, a personable young man in his early 30s. He was responsible for the catering function for the workshops. He would be punctually present every morning before the programme started to prepare beverages and snacks for the participants. He would then appear at mid-afternoon to do the same. He had a ready smile and greeting for me and every participant.

One day, I was telling the programme co-ordinator privately that we would give the class an earlier afternoon break that day because some participants needed to attend an urgent meeting. Benson apparently overheard. He quickly waltzed over to me and with his usual smile, asked: "Sir, should I bring the food up earlier this afternoon?"

I was already suspicious of Benson for a few days now. To me, a service worker who behaved like he enjoyed his work was a rare sight. But one who was proactive blew me away! The moment he asked me the question, I instinctively countered: "Are you the boss of the catering company?"

Benson was taken slightly aback. What had that to do with bringing up the food and drinks early? But when he saw that I was not giving up without an answer, he gingerly replied: "I am one of the partners."

He could have fooled me. He wore the same uniform as his employees. He worked like them and with them. It is refreshing to see how the boss brought himself down to work with his team.

Servant Leadership

I first came across this term "Servant Leadership" in 1990 when I was with ServiceMaster. It was an obscure concept. It is the title and subject of a book, published in 1977, written by the late Robert K. Greenleaf, an American corporate executive with AT&T. I had a hard time finding the book and finally got it at a small Christian bookstore.

Greenleaf defined Servant Leadership as:

"The servant-leader is servant first... It begins with the natural feeling that one wants to serve, to serve first. Then conscious choice brings one to aspire to lead. He or she is sharply different from the person who is leader first, perhaps because of the need to assuage an unusual power drive or to acquire material possessions. For such it will be a later choice to serve – after leadership is established. The leader-first and the servant-first are two extreme types..."

When I first encountered this principle, it hit me like a ton of bricks. What? A leader is a servant? I remember my orientation experience in ServiceMaster cleaning hospitals. At first, I did not understand how learning to clean toilets would help me in my management career with the company. But after a few months into my first assignment managing the support services of a hospital, a light bulb went off in my head. Having experienced the same work my staff did, I could empathise and guide them competently.

When one of them complained that a task could not be done, I was in a position to judge if this was true because I had done it myself. If true, I would work with that person to find a better way to get the job done. If not, I would be firm in asserting that the task be done. When a staff shared with me difficulties on the job, I could capably relate to what he/she was saying. Another plus of learning the work first-hand was my ability to chip in and help when workloads got too heavy or when there was a staff shortage. Nothing cheered people on more than when they saw their leader rolling up his/her sleeve and working alongside them. Just like Benson in the story before.

It dawned on me that my role as a leader was really to serve those who followed me. My job, at the end of the day, was to support and enable my staff to achieve their goals and potential. If they could do that, then my own goals, which were collective of theirs, were also met. It is about empowering and developing others to achieve together. According to Greenleaf, the best test of Servant Leadership is "do those you serve grow as persons: do they, while being served, become healthier, wiser, freer, more autonomous, more likely themselves to become servants?"

Please do not get me wrong. A Servant Leader is not a doormat for his/her followers to step on. It does not mean being submissive and relenting. Serving means keeping others accountable, giving directions and visions, and ensuring discipline. You are serving your subordinate when you set goals together with him/her and then constantly work with him/her to make sure the goals are accomplished. By doing all that, you are ultimately serving that person to ensure that the person grows and that the organisational objectives are met. Servant

Leadership is result-driven except that the results include both the organisation and the individual. Serving even extends to seemingly darker issues like firing people. But when an employee is terminated after an exhaustive due process, this person is liberated to seek his/her true calling elsewhere. In the longer run, this benefits both that person and the organisation.

But is Servant Leadership still obscure? Not anymore. It has gained prominence in the last few years, especially in the West. There is a shift in many organisations, both profit and non-profit, away from traditional autocratic and hierarchical models of leadership and towards Servant Leadership. To quote Larry Spears, the CEO of Greenleaf Center for Servant Leadership: "Servant Leadership seeks to involve others in decision-making, is strongly based in ethical and caring behaviour, and it enhances the personal growth of workers while improving the caring and quality of organisational life."

Servant Leadership forms the anchor to service excellence. When a leader sees oneself and the organisation as a servant to one's people and customers, you can bet your bottom dollar that service will shoot through the roof!

Crossroads

Back in the East, Servant Leadership is still struggling to find its way into the mainstream. This has a lot to do with our Asian values and practices. Servant Leadership preaches a bottom-up approach while many Asian organisations and homes are still class-conscious, patriarchal and autocratic in practice. To many Asians, the words "servant" and "leader" are usually thought of as opposites. "Servant" connotes lowly position, obedience, submission etc. "Leader" conjures images of authority, power, know-it-all etc.

Research shows that people tend to be more motivated to work harder if bosses relate to them like key persons from their past, usually parents. In a Harvard Business Review article from September 2004, Michael Maccoby, an American management consultant, observed that Westerners typically saw fathers and bosses as people who were helpful when needed but generally encouraged followers to be independent. By contrast, Asians generally viewed fathers and bosses as authority figures. Extending this to the workplace, they are used to and even prefer bosses to be protectors who can teach them and tell them what to do. They are programmed to not challenge authority.

This is where Asia is at a crossroad. As it continues to develop and modernise, Asians' expectations and thinking are slowly changing. Especially with the younger generation. Maccoby found a new trend: "Young managers from Beijing, where the Cultural Revolution broke traditional family patterns, responded somewhat like the Westerners. They described the ideal leader as a good basketball coach who put people in the right roles, promoted teamwork, and knew how to adapt strategy to changing competition."

The rise of individualism is evident now throughout Asia. As people become more affluent, their children are getting more pampered and freedom. The "little emperors" is a term used by the Chinese to describe their children in one-child families. These little emperors are growing up to expect more free will and space to assert themselves. The sociologists term them Generation Y, referring to people born after 1977. Generation Yers are self-confident, independent, and adaptable to change and technology. Leading them with the traditional top-down mode is disastrous. Instead, they want Servant Leaders who can nurture, guide and accommodate them.

The answer therefore lies in Servant Leadership that puts people in the centre. More can be achieved when leaders bring out the best in others by listening, empathising, coaching, involving, strategising, conceptualising and growing others. We are in the early stages yet. But Service Unusual organisations can get a head start by adopting this leadership style.

Principles of Servant Leadership

I believe that Servant Leaders subscribe to the following 3 principles:

1) People

A Servant Leader sincerely believes in the potential of people. He/She has an understanding of the diversity of people's gifts, talents and skills. This understanding enables the leader to trust people and admit that he/she does not know and cannot do everything. The growth and development of followers who do the work is the primary aim. When that happens, these employees will then see to it that the customer is served correctly and well and that the bottom-line is black.

James Heskett, Thomas Jones, Gary Loveman, Earl Sasser and Leonard Schelesinger developed the Service Profit Chain that shows the linkage between employee satisfaction and revenue/profitability. The premise is if the leaders take good care of employees with rewards/recognition, growth opportunities as well as proper working conditions and tools, the employees will tend to stay with the organisation and be productive. This will, in turn, result in better service quality and higher customer satisfaction and loyalty. Such customer endorsements will translate into higher revenues and profits that allow the organisation to invest more in its employees and internal service.

Power in the Service of Others

Believing in people is only the first step. This belief and trust should

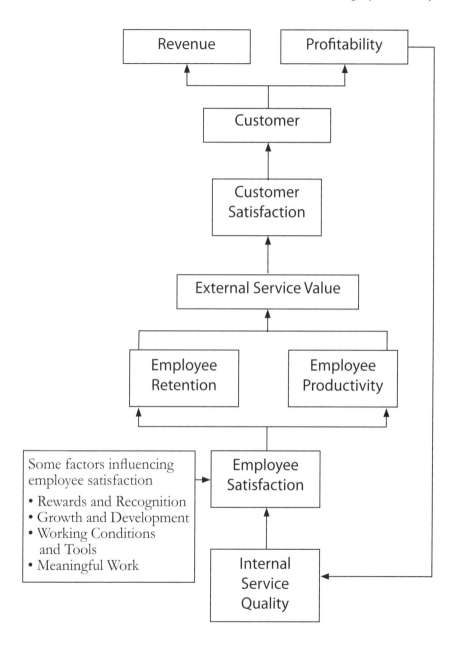

Service Profit Chain

then be acted out by sharing authority and power with the people in question. This is tough. People who feel powerless tend to hoard whatever shreds of power they have. Powerless managers tend to adopt petty and dictatorial management styles. Powerlessness creates politicking and selfishness. Yet power is expandable, not fixed. Power shared results in higher job satisfaction and performance. Meg Whitman, CEO of eBay, said in a recent interview: "I don't actually think of myself as powerful." She agreed that "to have power, you must be willing to not have any of it". It is about a reciprocity of influence: when power is shared, people, in turn, feel more strongly attached to the leader and more committed to effectively carrying out duties and responsibilities. When the leader strengthens others, his/her level of influence with them increases. The bottom line is: "You look good, I look good". The common reversal is "You must look bad for me to look good". Servant Leaders possess a spirit of humility. They have a strong sense of self-confidence. To Servant Leaders, service is "glamorous". They take pride in serving others. They are mature enough to give up power and status, to be proven wrong, and to let others take credit. Support and sharing of power do not result in the loss of control and discipline and becoming a populist. Instead, true support requires firmness and objectivity. Mahatma Gandhi, the "Bapu", or father, of modern India, was a humble man of small stature. He moved an entire nation by his quiet acts of self-reliance and his vision of non-violence. He did not move mountains with his speeches. He did not lead his people in a war. Through his understated leadership, India won its independence.

Credibility

"To be persuasive we must be believable; to be believable we must be credible; to be credible, we must be truthful," Edward R. Murrow, legendary American news journalist, once said.

Servant Leaders must possess and demonstrate strong moral values like Integrity, Honesty, Fair-mindedness, and Dependability etc. in order to win trust. These values define credibility, which is hard to earn and easy to lose. Hewlett Packard alerted customers in 2004 to a flaw in its notebooks: a defective chip that could trigger the loss of data. When asked why it had taken such a move that could dent its profit margin, a company spokesman said: "We want to be pro-active and offer help to customers who might be affected by it." Ethics are now commonly taught in business schools.

Best Practices of Servant Leaders

Next, let's translate these principles into practices. Servant Leaders are distinguishable by the following behaviours:

1) Advocate for Customer

When an organisation enjoys a reputation for treating customers royally, its leaders invariably speak of customer service as a philosophy or religion. Jack Welch and his top managers in General Electric made a point of personally meeting major customers twice a year. The Servant Leaders represent the voice of the customer in the organisation. When making decisions, they always ask the same questions: "What would our customers want or prefer?" or "What would our customers get out of this?" or "Would this benefit our customers?" They constantly encourage and inspire the staff to be customer-focused. They create and emphasise customer measures.

2) Walk-the-Talk

Servant Leaders do more than preach and philosophise. They make service strategies real through visible management. They exemplify for their employees what it means to produce great service. Richard Branson, the founder of Virgin Atlantic airline, doesn't sit in first class;

he will be walking up and down the aisles asking customers what they think of Virgin. He also takes an active interest in following up any letters of complaint that get directed to him. McDonald's requires all its top managers to spend time manning the service counters during induction and on an annual basis to understand what service staff and customers experience.

3) Insist on High Standards

One way Servant Leaders trust and support their employees is by setting astronomically high standards for them. Federal Express blazed the trail of guaranteeing absolutely, to deliver every package by 10:30am the next morning. When it comes to standards, Servant Leaders are uncompromising. Ray Kroc, founder of McDonald's, once visited a branch and noticed a crumpled napkin in the parking lot, a clear violation of McDonald's standards of cleanliness. He stormed into the outlet and fired the manager.

4) Empower Others

Servant Leaders sometimes go to extremes to get their people to act autonomously and take risks. The Ritz-Carlton Hotel allows employees to spend up to 2,800 Singapore dollars to resolve a customer problem without the need to seek approval. Getting people to take risks is a powerful way to improve efficiency. The bane of any customer service operation is the employee who says: "This is not my job," or "I have to ask my superior." By passing the problem to someone else, the employee not only alienates the customer but also multiplies the work the organisation must do to produce service.

5) Motivate and Inspire

Servant Leaders use an arsenal of motivational techniques to get employees to exceed customers' expectations. These techniques, like slogans, awards, meetings, form the visible symbols of the culture of the workplace. They reward and recognise heroic service acts. They tie compensation to service. They communicate and role-model the intended service values. They treat employees as they wish employees to treat customers.

So, what do you think of Servant Leadership? Does it make sense? Can it work in your organisation? Is it easy to adopt? If you are like most people, you will find leading by serving a logical and inspiring idea. But is it easy to follow? No. You will need to change your current mindset and habits. Are you prepared to seek input rather than tell? Are you willing to give up divisive perks like a private dining room to eat in the cafeteria with the rest of the people? Can you let your people loose and trust them to do the right thing? But before I start to discourage you, you and I know that as in any endeavour, mastery is a journey. It starts with a commitment to want to learn and change. Then take baby steps. Continue to be patient and persist even in the face of obstacles. Over time, all of us can become Servant Leaders.

Who Really Conquered Mount Everest?

We will close this chapter with a role model on Servant Leadership. This account is not set in a typical corporate setting. It takes place in a historical event: the first successful ascent of Mount Everest in 1953. I came across this account in the October 13th 2003 issue of the Fortune Magazine from an article, *The Board That Conquered Everest,* written by Michael and Jerry Useem. Below is my adaptation:

Most of us would have learnt of the first time men reached the top of the highest mountain in the world: Mount Everest. We would probably also know Edmund Hillary and Tenzing Norgay, the first men ever to achieve the feat. But as in every noteworthy endeavour, it takes a whole team of people to get the job done behind the scene.

This account takes us onto the back stage of this event.

Actually, Hillary and Norgay were not the first choice. Eric Shipton, a well-known English adventurer, was picked by the Royal Geographical Society for the attempt. Shipton had been involved in four previous expeditions to Everest and thus knew the mountain like no one else.

But not long after, the committee responsible for the expedition regretted the decision. Though Shipton was charismatic and popular, he was very disorganised. He tended to improvise a lot and paid scant attention to details and planning.

The team was working against time and competition. As recent as a year before, a Swiss team almost made it to the top of Everest. The Germans and French were watching closely.

Therefore six weeks after selection, Shipton was fired. This created an initial uproar. Many protested the firing. One member of the expedition backed out.

The committee realised that they needed a replacement who was result-oriented. He had to be the modern version of a leader: dedicated, humble, disciplined and diligent. He had to be a good planner, organiser and team builder. They found such a man in John Hunt. Hunt was a career military man. He was obsessed with details. For example, he specified that each box of ration contain 29 tins of sardines. No more, no less. He recognised that the expedition was a team effort. He demanded an "unusual degree of selflessness and patience". He later wrote: "The desire to reach the top must be both individual and collective."

Hunt was the opposite of Shipton. He was low-key and kept himself behind the scene. In fact when he was first chosen, many asked, including Hillary: "Who is this John Hunt?"

Hunt's goal was to get two climbers to the 29,035-foot summit. But there were 10 climbers were in the team. Hunt insisted that the final two climbers would depend on impartial factors like who were making the most progress at that time and were in the high camp when the weather turned conducive. In other words, the honour would go to the two who were at the right place at the right time.

The expected final two, Tom Bourdillon and Charles Evans, came within 300 feet of the summit. Unfortunately, at that stage, they ran out of stamina and sunlight. Yet, abiding by their leader Hunt's philosophy, they selflessly left behind a stash of oxygen canisters for others as they retreated. They also brought back and shared valuable information on their experience.

Hunt, ever vigilant, had already prepared supplies within 2000 feet of the summit for a backup team. On the morning of May 28, Hillary and Norgay moved out. The weather conditions on that night was terrible. Hunt's supplies helped them pull through. At 4am, they pushed on, carrying with them the remainder of Hunt's supplies: crackers, lemonade, a heating stove and ironically, the final tin of Hunt's sardines.

At 11:30am of May 29, 1953, the two men reached the summit. Hillary snapped the now-famous photo of Norgay with an ice axe raised in victory. From that moment on, the world knew of Hillary and Norgay. But we now know the truth. The accomplishment was more than just theirs.

Were Eric Shipton still in charge, he would probably make sure he was

John Hunt, Courtesy of Royal Geographic Society

the one in the photo at the summit. Perhaps till this moment, many of us have never heard of John Hunt, the true leader of this expedition. We need more John Hunts; leaders who are willing to serve and ensure the team achieves its goals. They do not begrudge others hogging the limelight and taking the credit.

There are actually many John Hunts in the world. They have substance but are not easily noticeable. Instead board of directors are enamoured with the Eric Shiptons; conventional leaders full of form and style.

Who conquered Mount Everest? If you ask me, John Hunt did!

Personal Practice Tips:

A Servant Leader:

- Champions the customers.
- Dirties his hands and works with the people.
- Manages by wandering around and not from a desk.
- Gives the benefit of the doubt to others: believes in the goodness of people.
- Gives people a second chance when plausible.
- Has respect for people.
- Knows people's names.
- Prefers listening more than talking.
- Involves others in decision-making.
- Constantly thinks of ways to make people more productive and how to reward them.
- Has no reserved parking space, private washroom or dining room.
- Keeps costs trim and yet willing to spend when called for.
- Has an open door policy.
- Tolerant of dissenting views and opinions.
- Delegates important jobs to others.
- Trusts others.
- Takes the blame when something goes wrong.
- Puts the spotlight on others instead.
- Gives credit to others.
- Gives honest, straightforward and frequent feedback.
- Knows when and how to fire people.
- Goes to where the trouble is to help and take responsibility.

- Prefers personal contacts to e-mails and phone calls.
- Admits mistakes, comforts others when they admit them.
- Promotes from within.
- Keeps promises.
- Always believing, referring to and living out the organisation's values.
- Sees mistakes as learning opportunities.
- Stays optimistic and encourages people to do the same.
- Is firm but fair.
- Is friendly but not overly familiar with others.
- Shows toughness and persistence in tackling nasty problems.
- Makes tough decisions.
- Hates bureaucracy, unnecessary controls and paperwork.
- Plans for successors.
- Coaches and mentors people constantly.
- Focuses on results and goals.
- Never asks others to do what own self is not willing to do.
- Always looks for ways to improve and value-add.
- Is proud of having and demanding high standards.
- Likes to think strategically and conceptualise broadly.
- Stays realistic and practical at all times.

SUMMARY

"I don't know what your destiny will be, but one thing I know, the only ones among you who will be really happy are those who have sought and found how to serve."

ALBERT SCHWEITZER, NOBEL PEACE PRIZE WINNER, 1952

A Calling for Passion

If you have come this far in the book, you are most likely keen to find your place in this service economy. You would like to move away from the rest of the pack. It is challenging, partly because the pack itself is running faster and smarter.

So how do you outshine this pack of service counterparts? If they are fast, you have to be faster. If they gain more power, you have to beef up even more. This is good but tiring. You have to keep moving and looking over your shoulders.

Is there a better way?

Who says that the only way to beat your competitors is to be better? You just have to be different. That's the main message of this book. Michael Dell never wavered in the face of detractors who sneered that no one would buy a computer before seeing and touching it. He is of singular mind when it comes to selling directly to end-users while others in his position would have been tempted to create other marketing channels.

The key differentiator is passion. You need passion to succeed in any endeavour. You have to see service as a calling and not work. You have to believe that service is a noble profession like any other. Service Master has an established research and development programme with chemists and physicists constantly coming up with better ways to clean and housekeep. Who would have thought that work as mundane as cleaning could be "professionalised"? The company produces technical manuals on floor mopping, carpet spotting etc. The staff cannot help but be proud of what they do when they are surrounded by such an emphasis on professionalism and quality.

While most of the pack sees service as a mere transaction, you can stand out if you and your people embrace service as what it should be: deriving fulfilment by genuinely giving yourself to help others. The recipients, your customers, can readily tell the passion in your behaviour, procedures and offerings.

Practices

Passion and Practicality need to go hand-in-hand. You can be totally convinced that you can fly on your own. You can then prove it to the world by jumping off the Petronas Towers in Kuala Lumpur. You will make the headlines but for the wrong reasons.

Passion has to be coupled with a healthy dose of realism that can be implemented and practiced. This book shares 10 practices that will help put you ahead of the pack:

Service **Unusual** Practice #1:
Stop benchmarking against others and become a benchmark for others.

There is little or no profit to ending up as generic commodities. Instead, go where no one is. Think counter-intuitive. Leave the pack. This does not mean going faster and growing bigger all the time. You just need to be different. This can even mean going slower or becoming smaller. To do that, you have to constantly question conventions. This practice serves as the guiding philosophy for the other nine practices.

Service **Unusual** Practice #2:
World-class service goes beyond providing solutions, to ensuring that the customer has a memorable experience being served.

Service is no longer just providing what the customers need and want. Customers are more sophisticated today and they are looking to leave the service transaction feeling right and good. Service therefore becomes a series of opportunities to create the desirable impression. If you can provide the right experience for your customers, your bankers will be delighted along with your customers.

To create a desirable experience, you are required to put in place several factors: Customers, Service Strategy, People, Process, Product, Measurement and Leadership. These must synergise to bring about the targeted outcome. The remaining practices are about these factors.

Service **Unusual** Practice #3:

Kick the habit of relying just on customer ratings. If we really want to know our customers, ask and listen for their qualitative feedback.

Relationship with your customers must be personalised. That means attaching importance to communicating with them directly. Ask them to tell you not just how they find your services but also what they expect from you in the future. Treat what they tell you as recipes to improve and innovate your services.

Service **Unusual** Practice #4

Customer complaints are useful. We should encourage our customers to complain more.

When you talk with your customers, you want to ask for areas of dissatisfaction, as they are the main source for improvements. You have to see complaints in a positive light. If so, the next challenge then is to get your customers to speak up.

Service **Unusual** Practice #5:

Customer Loyalty is Dead! Customers are only as loyal as the value they get from you.

You have to be on your toes constantly to ensure that you are offering your customers more benefits than what it costs them to experience your service. Not only that, this benefit-cost gap has to be greater than your competitors. If not, be prepared to bid your beloved customers farewell.

Service **Unusual** Practice #6:
There is no good service, only the right service. Right service is good service.

Service is downright subjective. One man's delight is another man's nightmare. The trick is therefore to focus and target a customer group that can appreciate the type of service you are competent to provide. Be famous for only what you are or can be good at. The danger is when you try to please too many people.

Service **Unusual** Practice #7:
We do not own our employees. We should focus on developing and retaining only those who can add value to us and to whom we can add value.

You are your employee's customer. You have every right to expect value add from the person. In return, the employee has the right to expect and obtain the desired benefits from you. Like any other customer relationship, work loyalty is dead. It is all about the right fit between employer and employee. The employee has to ultimately take charge of his/her own development.

Service **Unusual** Practice #8:
Our service processes and products should be designed "inside-out" with our people in mind so that they can be enabled to serve our customers better.

Be careful that you do not get carried away with putting in impressive systems and technology that might hinder your people's efficiency and effectiveness. Introduce processes and products that cater to both internal and external customers. A proven and simple way to do this is to failsafe potential service breakdowns before they occur. Though fail-safing is not new, this discipline is often neglected.

Service **Unusual** Practice #9:
We believe only in measures that can allow our people to buy in and make improvement to our performance.

Like process, you have to ensure that your people can accept your measurement system. The types of measures will depend on your service operations. The general rule-of-thumb is to do with as few measures and standards as possible without compromising reliability and consistency in your service.

Service **Unusual** Practice #10:
A leader is a servant to his/her followers.

Your leadership forms the anchor and foundation to your entire service offering. To lead in the 21st century, you need to learn how to serve. Your role as a leader is to support your people so that they can achieve their goals. By doing so, your goals are simultaneously accomplished.

AFTER
THOUGHT

To many organizations, service is not a new initiative. Many will tell you that they have expended much resource to try to bring up and sustain their desired service levels. Though very few have success stories to share, these organisations certainly cannot be faulted for lack of trying. They are working hard to win but they are not working smart enough to win.

Working smart requires us to take a more "laissez faire" approach to service. The practices in this book reflects this philosophy that the only the fittest will survive. These survivors are smart enough to know that they do not need to be "all things to all men". They place their attention on finding the right and most profitable customers for what they can best provide. They work hard to learn what these customers need and want. They then design the appropriate service processes to offer just the right level of service to these right customers. This philosophy applies also to their people. They focus on finding and keeping only the right people who can add value to them. They make sure these right staffs are well-taken off and they contribute greatly to the staffs' development and learning. They measure their performance to ensure that they are on track with their customers' aspirations and know what improvements need to be made. Their leaders walk the talk by putting service at the top of their agenda. These executives do so because they can equate service directly with returns.

Working smart is also ensuring that all components influencing service quality are aligned and integrated. Many organisations take the easy way by sending their people for training and upon their return expect them to transform automatically into service champions without subsequent guidance and coaching. Others go through the routines of putting in place the right environment, policies, procedures but are faced with under-motivated people and indifferent leaders. Such initiatives are well-intended but piecemeal. Therefore they do not work.

The intent of this afterthought is to organize and prioritise the 10 service unusual practices advocated in this book so that you can implement them in the right order. I use this sequence in my work with organizations seeking genuine service transformation. This sequence represents a holistic and integrated intervention that can bring about lasting service improvement

I group the 10 practices into 3 phases. The phases are iterative:

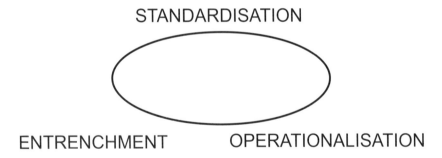

Standardisation

This phase involves determining and designing the right service. Its activities include:

- Understand the different segments of customers and what they need/want (Service Unusual Practice #3).

- Then determine the right service strategy and values for the selected customer segments (Service Unusual Practices #5 and #6).

- Design the appropriate service processes, policies, procedures and standards to bring about the desired service experience (Service Unusual Practices #2, #6 & #8).

Operationalisation

This phase is concerned with implementing the service strategy, processes and standards determined in the previous phase:

- Train the people to carry out the service processes and standards (Service Unusual Practice #7).

- Coach the leaders to be able to place service as a top priority and uphold the service standards (Service Unusual Practice #10).

- Coach and monitor the people to ensure the service standards are carried out. (Service Unusual Practices #7 and #10).

- Create frequent service campaigns and rallies to keep the motivation alive (Service Unusual Practice #10).

Entrenchment

This phase helps ensure that the service momentum continues:

- Seek feedback from customers for improvement (Service Unusual Practices #3 & #4).

- Determine the right service measures to evaluate the people (Service

Unusual Practice #9).

- Link rewards and recognition to the service measures (Service Unusual Practices #7 & #9).

- Revisit and update the service strategy to stay ahead. (Service Unusual Practice #1)

Applying the principles and practices of this book is going to be trying but exciting. Trying because it requires you to think and act differently from your peers. It will be a lonely journey as you move away from the pack. You will face obstacles and failures along the way. The practices discussed in this book involve discipline, going back to basics, focus, and accountability. These are values that the service world forgets sometimes.

Hence, from this point on, your resilience and determination will be called into play. Will you persist? If so, you will become unusual and successful. This journey never ends but you will continuously make progress if you press on. I will leave you with the words of Sir Winston Churchill, the British wartime statesman:

"Success is the ability to go from one failure to another with no loss of enthusiasm."

About the Author

George T.K. Quek has over 15 years of experience in the service industry, both as a senior corporate executive and a consultant. His career with Fortune 500 and regional organisations like ServiceMaster and Andersen Consulting spans many Asian countries: Singapore, Hong Kong, Taiwan, China, Thailand, Indonesia and Sri Lanka.

George was formerly the Director of Service Quality Centre, a subsidiary of Singapore Airlines that provides training and consulting solutions in the area of service excellence. In the last 5 years, he has trained, coached and consulted for over 3,000 executives from more than 80 organisations like Siemens, Deutsche Bank, Kasikornbank, Thailand AIS, SASIN Graduate School, Singapore Changi Airport, Inland Revenue of Singapore, Macau International Airport, Hong Kong Convention & Exhibition Centre and Dragonair.

George holds a MBA from The University of Texas at Austin. He is also a certified corporate coach and administrator of personality profiles like MBTI and DISC.

He is currently the founding director of DistincTions Asia Pte Ltd, a regional human capital and organisation development consulting company with offices in Singapore, Hong Kong and Thailand.

When not working, George enjoys his weekend golf outings and supporting his favourite soccer team, West Ham United.

He can be reached at george@distinctions-asia.com.

www.serviceunusual.com

This book serves as a stepping-stone to your ultimate goal of providing a Service Unusual. The ball is now in your court: the onus is on you to put what you have learnt into practice. As you apply these practices, you will experience pain and joy. These experiences can benefit others too, by helping them to reduce their own learning curves. To this end, I have created a website to complement this book. Its purpose is to provide a platform for a community of service unusual champions and exponents who are willing to selflessly share best practices with one another. I encourage you to be part of this community. All you have to do is to visit the website and register your interest. In return, you will receive regular updates and sharing of service unusual tips and experiences.

Other Publications

Handbook For Businessmen - Doing Business In Singapore

Goh Tianwah   ISBN 981-052974-0   Price: S$24.00   2005 Edition

Do you know if you need special licences to operate a certain business?

Do you need to insure your employees under the Workmen's Compensation Act?

What are your duties and responsibilities as a director in your company?

The answers to these questions and many more are found in this book.

Handbook For Businessmen is a one-stop guide for anyone starting a business. It gives you the vital information you need on all aspects of business from domain name registration, business and company registration, business licences, government grants and assistance schemes to employment regulations in Singapore.

It will help you navigate through the maze of information and issues of doing business in Singapore. It will point you to the right agencies and government departments for your business needs. Topics covered in the book include:

- Types Of Business Structure And Their Implications – Sole Proprietorship, Partnerships, and Companies
- Internet, Domain Names And Your Business
- Tax Incentives For Foreign Investors
- Foreign Entrepreneurs And Employment Of Foreigners
- Guide To The Companies Act
- Guide To Taxation In Singapore
- Employment Regulations – The Employment Act, The Workmen's Compensation Act, The Part-time Employment Act and CPF Regulations
- Assistance Schemes And Grants For SMEs

GUIDE TO LETTERS OF CREDIT
By Goh Tian Wah
Price: S$23.00

ISBN 981-04-3969-5

A practical guide for importers, exporters, bank staff, and those involved in handling documentary credits and financing of international trade. It has been revised and updated with accordance with the new Uniform Customs and Practice For Documentary Credits (1993 Revision No. 500).

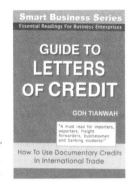

The book covers:

•The Nature Of Documentary Credit •Types of Documentary Credits • Banking Practices For Documentary Credit •Uniform Customs and Practice for Documentary Credits • How To Comply With The Credit Terms • Negotiation of Credits • How To Ensure Accurate Documentation • How To Deal with Discrepancies • Finance of Overseas Trade • Maritime Fraud

Export Import Procedures & Documentation
By Goh Tian Wah
Price: S$18.00

ISBN 981-04-2312-8

Thoroughly revised, this book offers students, businessmen and practitioners a comprehensive look at import and export procedures and documentation in Singapore. It is also useful to those involved in shipping, purchasing operation, freight forwarding and distribution.

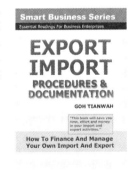

Topics include:
1. **Incoterms In International Trade**
2. **Methods of Payment**
3. **Shipping Procedures**
4. **Import and Export Procedures:** The Inward and Outward Declaration forms; list of goods under export or import controls customs requirements; customs duties and duty drawback claim procedures etc.

Reaching Your Child The Right Way through Learning Styles

By Michael Choy

Edition 2004

Price: S$11.00

ISBN 981-05-0984-7

Reaching Your Child The Right Way through Learning Styles describes ways to better manage your child's behaviour. You, the parent, will cultivate methods of shaping your child's manners and learn how to deal with misbehaviour more effectively using simple rules and consequences. Practical tips found in this book will help you to be a more effective parent and raise a better-behaved child.

This book covers amongst other topics:
- Various learning styles and understanding your child's style,
- Effective rules-setting and enforcement,
- Principles of rewarding good behaviour, and
- The importance of being a role model for your child.

Discipline Techniques That Work!

Michael Choy has gathered practical examples and techniques from his teaching experience and his research into educational issues to help you nurture your child in the critical years.
Ex-teacher with more than 20 years' experience and parent

This little book is a nugget of wisdom. I am especially heartened with its closing emphasis on parental role modeling and its inclusion of caring as a viable option for discipline.
Dr Tay Eng Guan, Assistant Professor
National Institute of Education

Success With Small Business
By Chan Pak Chuen
Price:S$19.00   ISBN 981-04-6747-8

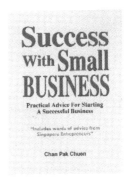

Filled with real case studies and lots of practical advice, this book helps new business owners navigate their road to success. Readers will gain a clear perspective of what they should do every step of the way towards starting their own business. Includes advice from successful entrepreneurs in Singapore.

The Power of Relationships
By Patrick Low Kim Cheng
Price:S$19.00   ISBN 981-04-4045-6
(Published By BusinesscrAFT Consultancy)

The *Power of Relationships* will show you how you can empower yourself with the relationship edge in order to achieve success in business, at work and in your personal life.

Contract Law For Business People
By Suchitthra Vasu
Price:S$19.00   ISBN 981-04-3712-9

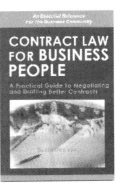

This book is written for businessmen, managers and executives. It provides you with a concise understanding of the law of contract and tips for drafting better contracts. You will learn how to draft various types of contracts including distributorship and agency agreements for those involved in international trade.

Topics covered include:
• The Nature, Definitions and Formation of Contracts
• Breach of Contract
• Termination of Contract • Private International Law
• Contracts in the World of e-Commerce
• Tips for Drafting Better Contracts • Contract for the Sale of Goods

Neo Presentation Plus

Neo Presentation allows you to create interactive e-Learning lessons in minutes using simple PowerPoint files. It integrates sound, video, music and flash animation graphics to create dynamic multimedia content for distribution on the Internet, intranet, LAN and on CD Rom.

Now, anyone can create impressive presentations and training materials, with no need for a programming background. Neo Presentation is the solution to creating high quality interactive training materials at the lowest cost. Its revolutionary Text-To-Speech feature uses the voice of a native English speaker for a more realistic audio learning experience.

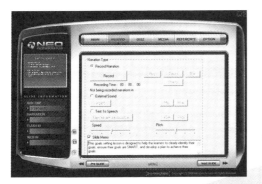

Neo Presentation Is The Ultimate E-Learning Authoring Tool For Businesses, Educators, Subject Matter Experts & Trainers!

Save time and increase productivity by creating e-Learning lessons quickly for your training needs

Enjoy the benefits of e-Learning, whilst minimizing implementation and development costs

Increase sales by creating spectacular multimedia sales presentations to win customers

Easy distribution of contents for learners to access anywhere, anytime (using the Internet, Intranet, LAN, PCs & laptops).

Easy to Install and simple to use. Create professional presentations in minutes!

Neo Presentation Plus Makes It So Easy To Meet Your Training Needs. Get more for less by calling Rank Books now!

Features:

- Rapidly converts powerpoint slides into interactive Flash format
- Realistic and built-in TTS (Text To Speech) feature voice narration
- Built-in support for graphics, audio, video and flash animation
- Includes questions and quiz generator with automated tracking and results

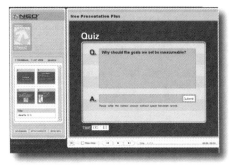

Graphic and multimedia handling:

- Supports .jpg and .gif graphics
- Supports audio and video streaming
- Macromedia Flash elements
- Preview window for browsing media objects (graphics, audio, video)

Main Functions

- Insertion of narration or external wav files
- TTS (Text To Speech) and Standard Narrations
- Biography information
- Reference and data links
- Bookmarks and email sending
- Quiz (Multiple choice, Yes/No, Short answer)
- Animation effects and set timings
- User choice volumes of files
- Preview and list selection
- Data searching
- View slide notes
- Two options for changing slides
- Display company logo

PC Environment

- Microsoft Windows 98 or above
- IBM compatible PC with Pentium 200MHz
- 64MB main memory or more (recommended: 128MB or higher)
- CD-ROM drive
- "1024 X 768"Graphic card, 16bit or more
- Sound card
- Mouse

Call Us For A Demo Of Neo Presentation Plus Today!

Contact Rank Books at 6250 8180
Fax: 6250 6191
Email: admin@rankbooks.com

Rank Books Blk 1002 Toa Payoh Ind Pk #07-1423 Singapore 319074